D1461425

Recruiting
for
Results

Recruiting
for
Results

*How to grow the business by
hiring the best performers*

STEVE KNEELAND

How To Books

105,452
£9-99

First published by How To Books Ltd, 3 Newtec Place,
Magdalen Road, Oxford OX4 1RE, United Kingdom.
Tel: (01865) 793806. Fax: (01865) 248780.
email: info@howtobooks.co.uk
http://www.howtobooks.co.uk

British Library Cataloguing in Publication Data.
A catalogue record for this book is available from
the British Library.

Edited by David Venner
Cover design by Shireen Nathoo Design
Cover image by PhotoDisc

Produced for How To Books by Deer Park Productions
Typeset by Kestrel Data, Exeter
Printed and bound by Cromwell Press Ltd, Trowbridge, Wiltshire

NOTE: The material contained in this book is set out in good
faith for general guidance and no liability can be accepted
for loss or expense incurred as a result of relying in particular
circumstances on statements made in the book. Laws and
regulations are complex and liable to change, and readers should
check the current position with the relevant authorities before
making personal arrangements.

Contents

Preface

This book is designed to achieve one very specific goal – and that is to hire people who will come on board, or move into the new job, and deliver outstanding performance.

The amount of time and money which a company invests in bringing a new person up to speed – and the amount of time that you as a *manager* have to invest – is considerable. And the difference between hiring someone who turns out to be an *average* performer versus hiring someone who turns out to be an *outstanding* performer, in terms of the actual results achieved, is substantial. So there's an awful lot at stake.

And yet – hiring people is something that a lot of us don't really enjoy and most of us haven't really been trained to do. We do the best we can, and we put a lot of time into interviewing candidates and making our final hiring decision, but it is usually not a nice, tidy process and we rarely come to the end of it feeling completely confident that we have hired someone who is going to be an outstanding performer.

Our goal in this book is to change that. To make the whole process a bit more systematic. A bit more logical. To give ourselves a clear strategy for the interview, a set of practical tools to use, and a coherent framework within which to assess what various candidates have to offer.

A good book – like a good movie – springs from the collaborative efforts of a number of people.

I would like to extend a heartfelt thank-you to the fine people at Johnson & Johnson Medical Products, in Canada, for whom a great deal of the material in this book was originally developed. Special thanks too must be directed to Susan McTavish, the forward-thinking head of the human resources area who has since moved on to exciting new challenges at the company's corporate offices in Texas.

To Pam, my wife – to Jessica and Jennifer, our two daughters – my grudging recognition of their forebearance and support. I am still not convinced that moving me and my computer out to the garden shed was absolutely necessary.

To Giles Lewis, the missionary force behind How To Books, and Nikki Read, the person whose job it is to turn otherwise good ideas into coherent and readable books, my sincere thanks for their professional assistance, encouragement, and patience.

Credit having been given where credit is due, you the reader may now judge the book by its merits and blame me for anything you don't like about it.

Steve Kneeland

1

Taking a Behavioural Approach

In this book, we're going to look at an easier way of interviewing. We can't go back and we can't jump ahead to watch people on the job for which they are being considered as a candidate.

But we can come pretty close.

A BETTER WAY

Let's imagine that we're interviewing John Harris, currently a sales representative with Acme Copiers Limited, a candidate for a similar selling role within our own firm.

John's on the 'short list', having survived the first round of preliminary interviews. We'll be wanting to make some very pragmatic predictions about how he might perform if we decide to bring him on board.

What we're saying is that hiring John Harris would be relatively easy if we could do one of two things – or both:

- Observe John's past performance: Actually go back in time and watch John perform his day-to-day duties at Acme Copiers.

- Observe his future performance: Leap ahead into the future and observe John in action as a sales representative in our own company.

We're going to conduct the interview in such a way that lets us come as close as is humanly possible to actually 'seeing' that person in action. We're going to take a **behavioural** approach to the interview.

This means digging for the behavioural specifics of what happened in a situation. If our candidate, John, says that he convinced a customer to introduce a new product on a trial basis, taking a behavioural approach to the interview involves zeroing in on that incident and finding out what exactly happened. How the proposal was introduced, how the customer reacted initially, how that was actually *said* or *expressed*, how John responded, what happened next . . .

By way of illustration, let's listen in on an interview that's already underway. The interviewer, Susan Miller, is asking John Harris about his previous selling experience with Acme Copiers.

> Susan: 'You just mentioned that you were able to bring in a number of new accounts while you were selling for Acme even though you were only there for a few months. Do you think we could talk a little more about that?'
> John: 'It wasn't really very complicated, to tell the truth. The company names were given to me by my supervisor, and I was simply the one to make the initial contact.'
> Susan: 'What sort of guidance were you given? Did you and your supervisor sit down together, for example, and decide how best to make the initial approach?'
> John: 'Not really. That was something I had to work out for myself. And I just used what I thought was good common sense.'
> Susan: Tell me a bit more, if you could, about what strategies you used – and why you felt they were appropriate.'

Susan's obviously digging and probing. Trying to work her way past the candidate's general descriptions and ferret out what was actually done. By whom and why.

She will continue to dig, on that same specific point, until she's satisfied that she's got all the facts of this particular situation.

John, for his part, isn't being defensive. He's just doing what most people tend to do when they're in an interview – and that's to sum things up in pretty general terms. Which is understandable. There's an awful lot that one could say about oneself and one's career, and only a limited time in which to say it.

There's an almost universal tendency on both sides to want to cover too much ground in the interview lest some portion of the candidate's background isn't adequately covered. The end result is an interview that gathers general descriptions from the candidate but doesn't really delve beyond them. Let's refer to this as the 'horizontal' approach to interviewing.

Using the vertical approach

What top interviewers do is take a vertical approach. One that digs down to the level of actual behaviour. Actual quotations. He said this and then I said that.

They don't talk in generalities. If the candidate says that one of their main achievements during the past year was landing the ABC account, the top interviewer digs for the behavioural specifics:

- 'How is it that you targeted this specific account in your prospecting?'

- 'What was the nature of your initial approach to them?'

- 'Why did you do it that way?'

- 'What reaction did you get?'

- 'When you went in to see them, what did you do to prepare yourself?'

- 'Whose idea was it to bring the Director of Finance into the second meeting?'

And so on. *Who? What? When? Why? How?*

Like a newspaper reporter, the successful interviewer digs for the specifics of what happened. Landing the ABC account means little in and of itself. What counts is *how* it was done. It is the candidate's behaviour that tells us what sort of performance we can expect if we bring the person on board. It is this performance, not the landing of the ABC account, that we are hiring. Everything boils down to behaviour:

- The closer we come to assessing behaviour in the hiring process, the more solid will be the foundation of the decision we make, the *easier* will be the decision, and the more *confident* we will feel about the decision we make.

- The further we stray from assessing behaviour in the interview, the more tenuous will be the foundation for our decision, the harder it will be to make that decision, and the less confident we will feel about it after it has been made.

SPOTTING PERSONALITY PATTERNS

There are patterns in people's behaviour that are the basis of our whole approach to predicting future performance. Let's say you had a good friend you have known for quite a few years and you were asked to predict how that friend might do in the role of Press Liaison Officer for this year's local charity drive.

Your answer might well be:

'Jane will work very hard, she'll certainly show an awful lot of enthusiasm and she'll relate very well to other people. But she's not a very organised sort of person and someone will have to keep an eye on how she handles the paperwork and schedules her time.'

You'll say it *confidently*, you'll be comfortable with your prediction. And, more likely than not, your prediction will turn out to be an accurate and very perceptive one.

Now why does that seem easy when deciding whether to bring John Harris on board can be so difficult? There are a couple of reasons.

The first is that you *know* Jane whereas you've never met John Harris prior to your interview with him. You've actually *seen* what sort of results she was able to produce. You're not having to go out on a limb on the basis of what Jane said about herself.

But it's more than this. It's not just that you have had a chance to actually observe her behaviour. It's that you've seen *patterns* in that behaviour. Certain ways she has of handling situations, or relating to other people, or organising her activities. And you assume that those patterns will continue to show themselves in the future. You are predicting what she will do in the future on the basis of what she has done in the past.

And this assumption you're making is generally a safe one. There are certain things about people which usually *don't* change and Jane's tendency to be a bit disorganised is one of those things.

All this illustrates a very important point. One, in fact, that is the very foundation of our whole approach to selecting people. The point is this:

a person's future behaviour is best predicted on the basis of those habits and patterns which have characterised his or her behaviour in the past.

Let's expand upon that a bit.

MAKING THREE BASIC ASSUMPTIONS

When you predicted how Jane would do in the role of Press Liaison Officer, you were operating on the basis of three very critical assumptions. Putting them into practice is the heart of what genuinely skillful interviewing is all about:

- There are patterns in people's behaviour.

- They can be seen in past performance.

- And they will be there in the future.

1. There are patterns in people's behaviour
If we look closely at the behaviour of a person, a number of patterns begin to emerge.

They may avoid taking risks, show sensitivity in dealing with people, be a bit careless with detail, tackle problems aggressively, or have difficulty standing back and seeing the forest through the trees.

The pattern won't *always* be there. A person who is aggressive and domineering by nature may not act that way when dealing with a visiting director from head office. An individual who is detail-minded by nature will hopefully be experienced enough to know when *not* to worry about crossing t's and dotting i's. The sensitive manager will know when to get 'tough' with someone.

Still, a person's basic behavioural tendencies will never be too far from the surface. They will be there in the background, always pressing to get out.

2. They can be seen in past performance
If you look closely enough at a person's past performance, you'll see the patterns showing through. At times, they'll be obvious but at other times we'll have to dig pretty deep.

We'll notice how one person has been consistently cautious and conservative in making career moves or how another has tended to flourish in turnaround-type situations.

We'll see connections, too. The meticulous person who's good with detail may also wander from the original question. The person who is aggressive in their dealings with people may tend to tackle problems aggressively when faced with a subtle or complex problem for which there is no simple or direct solution.

The person who is good at organising things at work will probably tend to be well-organised at home as well. You'll see it in how they organise a swimming party for the kids or how they organise an upcoming holiday.

3. And they will be there in the future

Here's another important point. These patterns of behaviour don't usually change unless something very deliberate is done to change them. Even then, they seem to hang in there tenaciously.

Someone who's a perfectionist at the age of twenty-two will probably still be one at the age of eighty-two. The young lad who bullied the other kids in the schoolyard will probably end up being a boss who brow-beats his subordinates.

Those patterns will still be there next year. They may show up in a somewhat different way. But the basic patterns will still be there.

And this is the key to selecting people. We are relying on the fact that these basic patterns seldom change and that what a person has done in the past is, therefore, the best predictor of what he or she will do in the future.

THE CONCEPT OF PERSONALITY

Let's bring in the word 'personality' to refer to the sum total of the patterns we might observe in a person's behaviour or performance.

If someone is an active community leader, orders restaurant waiters around authoritatively, keeps a tight rein on their family's spending, barks at their dog, and tells us – in the interview – that they enjoy being in a position of authority over other people . . . then it's pretty obvious that the word 'dominant', a 'personality' term, would not be out of place.

We are saying that there is something *internal* in their make-up which tends to express itself consistently in the form of 'dominant' responses to individual situations.

It's not really important whether we think of the word 'dominant' as applying to the patterns themselves or to what's causing them. It amounts to basically the same thing.

In either case, we assume that there is an underlying source of continuity in a person's behaviour that produces patterns that allow us to predict the future on the basis of what we know about the past.

So now have a 'personality' that underlies the individual's past performance and that will, presumably, show up again in their future performance. If we had to draw a picture of it, it might look something like what you see in Figure 1.

The person's past performance and future performance turn out to be two tips of the same iceberg and personality is the bridge between the two.

PREDICTING THE FUTURE

Our basic strategy for predicting the future is illustrated in Figure 1. It involves going through three distinct steps every time we interview.

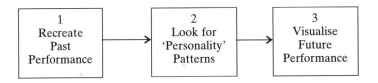

Fig. 1. Our strategy for predicting the future.

1. Recreate past performance

Using the candidate's description as our only guide, we have to re-create past behaviour until we can almost 'see' it unfolding in our own mind's eye. In effect, we use the candidate's description as a doorway to the past and go through it.

And that means digging and probing. Breaking through the barrier of the candidate's generalisations and interpretations and getting at the behavioural facts of what actually happened. Who said what to whom. How was it said and what happened next.

2. Look for 'personality' patterns

You'll find them if you've done a good enough job of getting the behavioural facts.

A good interviewer is always operating on two levels. On the behavioural or *performance* level to unearth the facts of what really happened and on the *personality* level to search for patterns.

And they attach words to them. They move from saying 'He did such-and-such' – an observational fact – to saying 'He *tends* to do such-and-such' – an inferential conclusion . . . from saying this is what he *did* to saying this is what he's *like*. He works well under stress. He looks at things methodically.

This is the 'inner world' of interviewing. A rarefied space that many of us never get to operate in. But it's here that the really good interviewers stop just gathering information and start doing something with it.

3. Visualise future performance

This final step involves projecting what we've learned about the person into the future. Not logically but *visually*.

Imagine them sitting in on the Tuesday morning staff meeting, or handling that sales call that you watched someone botch up yesterday afternoon, or standing in the booth beside you at next month's trade show in Madrid.

You can only create the future if you've systematically and consciously gone through the first two steps. Do it properly and the more vivid and the more useful will be the image that emerges from the third.

STRATEGY VERSUS TECHNIQUE

It is more important that you go away with this simple, three-step strategy firmly embedded in your mind than to send you away armed with a plethora of neat interviewing 'techniques'. It's more important that you understand the *process* – that you see the common-sense *logic* involved.

You could probably put this book aside right now because your approach to the interview, your *strategy*, would be a bit different.

Indeed, if this is all we did – take a behavioural approach to our interviewing of candidates – we would be better interviewers and we would do a better job of making decisions about people.

It would happen because we would have 'seen' the person in action. We would know what we were getting.

The really top interviewers, as it turns out, don't stop here. They go one step further.

2

Pinning Down What's Needed

It is not enough to simply predict a person's behaviour. To make a hiring decision, we also need to know whether that behaviour is what's needed for a successful performance on the job.

We need to know what behavioural patterns we are looking for. We need to know what specific patterns of behaviour will lead to success in the job – and which will be harmful or irrelevant.

It's a crucial question that each manager has to ask themself. What *are* the key things which make for successful performance in this job? In this particular division or this particular region of the country and under me as a manager.

In short, what are the specific things I should be looking for when I interview and then evaluate a candidate for the job?

TARGETED INTERVIEWING

The second part of our strategy for the interview involves taking a **targeted** approach to the interview.

Targeted means that we dig for behavioural specifics in a selective fashion. Our goal is to 'watch' the candidate perform in certain areas or in relation to certain situations. We need to get to the essence of what we mean by outstanding performance – in *this* company, in *this* segment of the business, with *you* as the manager.

So the question becomes – What do the top people in this job actually do? What is it about how they actually do things on a day-to-day basis that accounts for their being our top performers?

STARTING WITH THE JOB DESCRIPTION

Let's start with the **job description**. It's the logical place to start in our effort to pin down what's needed in the job.

If it's like most job descriptions, it will outline the key duties and responsibilities involved in the job as well as the reporting relationships, number of people supervised, and – perhaps – the goals that have to be achieved or the performance standards that must be satisfied.

Identifying knowledge and skills

There will usually be a description of what the job *requires* in the way of knowledge, skills, and job-related qualities. And it is in this section that we are most likely to find clues as to what we should be targeting in our interview.

Let's start with the most tangible and clear-cut of these items – the knowledge and skill factors.

Knowledge factors

Most jobs require a certain level of what might best be called technical knowledge or 'expertise'. It might be a knowledge of standard costing systems, or electronic circuitry, or it might be quite a bit broader . . . a good grasp of business fundamentals or a good basic understanding of how to manage people.

When people trip up due to lack of knowledge, it is typically in these latter areas – the broad ones. They have an insufficient grasp of business principles. They have an inadequate insight into their customer's business. They don't really understand what people in other departments within their own company are doing.

Skill factors

Skills, like knowledge, aren't directly observable, but we *can* see them being used – or not being used. By examining each of the areas of responsibility on a job description, it is usually not too difficult to list what skills are going to be needed.

Planning skills, analytical skills, conceptual skills, presentation skills, the skills of persuasion and leadership . . . are of increasing importance in most jobs. Sometimes there will be additional skills – project management skills, systems analysis skills, mechanical skills – which are quite specific and technical in nature.

When people trip up, it's not usually due to a lack of 'technical' skills. More often than not, it's the broad and intangible skills that are the culprit.

FOCUSING ON BEHAVIOUR

Our focus throughout this book is going to be on how to hire people who can come in and give us not just *acceptable* performance but *outstanding* performance.

Knowledge and skill factors, by and large, are minimum standards. Their presence will in most cases not be a guarantee of outstanding performance but their absence might be an *obstacle* to outstanding performance.

So we'll use them primarily as a means of sorting out the people we should interview versus those who'll be relegated to the back burner or rejected as un-qualified.

We need something that gets at what *outstanding* performance in the job is all about. The job description tells us that the ideal candidate will be a good communicator, a good team player, will be able to work effectively with minimal direction and will be an ambitious person who wants to get ahead in life.

But just how helpful are these statements? They sound rather general. Again, let's talk strategy.

We've already established that our approach to assessing what a candidate can do is going to be to focus on past behaviour. It makes sense, then, to retain the same behavioural focus when it comes to defining what we're looking for. What sort of *behaviour* are we looking for? That's going to be the question.

The job description as it stands probably doesn't tell us how the ideal incumbent should *behave*. The general prescriptions it contains – should be a good team player and have good communication skills – are not quite explicit enough to be deemed *behavioural*.

We're going to need to do something a little bit out of the ordinary.

LOOKING AT WHAT PEOPLE ACTUALLY DO

To describe behaviour we have to start by **looking** at what sort of behavioural patterns are needed in a job and the most logical thing to do is look at the behaviour of people already *in* that job.

So, at this juncture, we ask two very important questions:

- What are the specific behaviours that I see in my people that accounts for them producing good results? What specific behaviours do I see that I wish *everyone* would display?

105,452

- What specific behaviours do I see in my people which appear to *impede* successful performance?

Once we identify the bits and pieces of behaviour that spell the difference between outstanding and average performance, we begin sorting them into meaningful patterns and finding a name for each pattern.

Let's imagine, for example, that we're managing a team of internal IT consultants serving the needs of system users throughout our organisation. Meetings with internal customers are critical. In thinking about what makes our top people successful, we might notice that they all seem to do the following:

- They take a half-hour at the outset of the day to think about what lies ahead and sort out the priorities.

- They spend at least a half-hour thinking ahead and preparing for any important meeting.

- They go into a meeting with a clear agenda that has been written down somewhere on paper.

- They have thought through their answers to key questions that they might be expected to deal with.

- They know what they want to come away with – what *outcomes* they want to achieve.

Clearly, there's a *pattern* here. My top people seem to do a good job of planning. So I'll call it that – *planning*. Planning is one of the things that I have to look for and I'll give high marks to candidates who do the same sort of planning that I see my top performers doing.

DON'T BE LAZY

Someone has gone to the trouble of thinking about the job and putting together a list of the performance characteristics that are going to be important.

My advice is this – take it with a pinch of salt. Treat the list as a useful starting point. Go out there and see for yourself what specific behaviours are producing ourstanding results and what specific behaviours are *impeding* top-level performance.

Good communication skills? You don't have to look any further than Rita Malone:

- She's good at making small talk and getting people to relax, but she doesn't overdo it.

- She makes a point by giving you the overview first, then the details, and then she goes back and reiterates the overview.

- She actually made Jacques Beaudoin *smile* the other day. That's got to be a first.

- She can be gung ho and bubbly when talking to the sales people and yet be very businesslike, even downright *analytical*, when dealing with our technical people.

These behaviours are a large part of what accounts for her being an outstanding performer. She didn't just make Jacques smile – she got him to go along with the very same proposal that he rejected out of hand just a month ago.

So, if Rita's job is the one that we're hiring for, then communication skills are a must. And – looking at what Rita does – we know good communication skills when we see them.

LET'S NOT OVERSIMPLIFY THINGS

We're emphasising that we analyse what makes our successful people successful and then look for those characteristics in the people we hire.

Still, there's a potential problem in this approach if it is applied too literally. So let's take a moment to talk about it. Here are the pitfalls:

- The pattern is rarely a clear-cut one.

- People can compensate for shortcomings.

- A good quality can be carried too far.

- What's needed can change.

- Technical specs can be over-emphasised.

The pattern is rarely a clear-cut one

If we look at virtually any job, we will find certain skills that simply have to be there. An order entry clerk has to have basic keyboard skills. A sales representative has to have a certain level of persuasive skill. With them, a person has a chance. Without them, they should not be hired.

Once we go beyond the obvious, however, it is never really possible to pin down *exactly* what any given job requires for successful performance. In the case of most jobs the top performers tend to be rather unique in how they achieve their results. They may be alike in certain respects, but not to the point where one can say that there is a single definitive *model* that defines successful performance.

People can compensate for shortcomings

Even if we knew for sure that a certain skill was needed for success in a particular job, we would still have to be careful. People have a way of making up in one area what they may be lacking in another.

A person may be quite average when it comes to being a 'self-starter' but may achieve outstanding results through good planning and faultless organisation when working with clearly-defined goals and well-established guidelines.

A good quality can be carried too far

This is another and more subtle danger. A desirable characteristic – be it assertiveness or concern for detail – can begin to have not-so-desirable consequences if taken too far.

In searching for the person with assertiveness, we may inadvertently hire the one who irritates people with their aggressiveness and inability to listen.

Every strength can become a liability if carried to extremes or used inflexibly without regard for the demands of the situation at hand.

So we have to be very careful here. Yes . . . we want the candidate to be a self-starter but how *much* of a self-starter?

What's needed can change

A common error is to hire the person needed to solve yesterday's problems rather than the one needed to take advantage of tomorrow's opportunities.

The person we hire *this* year will have to be better than most of the ones we might have hired three years ago. And the ingredients needed to produce outstanding performance in the job will not be the same as the ingredients we were looking for back then. The total business environment in which we have to do our managing has become much more volatile, much more complex than it used to be.

What's needed can also *vary*. A laid-back style might produce good results in one region of the country whilst a more aggressive approach might be just what's needed in another.

Technical specs can be over-emphasised

A common hiring error is that of placing too much emphasis on technical qualifications or specific experience. People usually succeed or fail in a job for reasons which have more to do with operating style and interpersonal skills than with technical skills or knowledge.

Technical qualifications and specific experience should be used as criteria in the broad screening phases of the selection process, not as a reason for hiring or not hiring.

ASSESSING HOW THIS PERSON WILL ACTUALLY PERFORM

There's another, more subtle danger involved in drawing up lists of specific qualities and credentials that we feel a candidate's got to have.

We make the mistake of worrying too much about the sort of person we are *looking for* – rather than what sort of person we've got sitting in front of us.

Many interviewers spend too much time looking to see how a given candidate matches the 'specs' – rather than trying to get a feel for how each candidate would actually perform the job if given the opportunity.

Choosing people should be a lot like wandering into a cafeteria and deciding what to eat. You know you're hungry. But you don't really know what it is you wish yo eat. And you won't know until you've had a chance to browse around a bit, take a sniff or a nibble here and there before responding to what's on the menu.

Interviewing people should be an exciting job but it can't be if all you're doing is sifting through bodies until you find one that matches the 'specs'.

When you interview a candidate, focus all your energies and attention on discovering how that specific person will function, how they will do the job.

Don't worry – not during the interview – about *evaluating* their predicted performance. Focus all of your attention on *predicting* it.

ASSUMING THEY'VE BEEN HIRED

Assume they've been hired. Focus all of your attention on *how* they are actually going to perform.

But if we're going to assume that the person has been hired, why do we have to worry about pinning down what's needed to *do* the job?

Because it operates in the background. It sharpens our instincts. It gives the little black box inside us something to chew on.

It's like buying a house. It's helpful to sit down and make a list, on paper, of the various things that you want or don't want in a house. It's helpful to be as specific as possible – so that you can almost close your eyes and *picture* the house and walk around inside it.

But then you can throw out the list. It has done its job. Your subconscious has stored the criteria away somewhere, and your instincts will draw upon them judiciously when it comes time to react to an *actual* house.

That's the way the mind works.

3

Identifying the Ingredients for Success

Our approach to the interview, we have said, is going to be both **behavioural** and **targeted.**

The behavioural part is a second-best alternative. The ideal would be to go back in time and actually *watch* our candidates perform in a previous job. We can't do that, but we'll come as close as we can by digging for behavioural specifics during the interview.

What about the second part of our strategy. Targeted. Targeted at what? We have said that, when we watch a person perform, we instinctively compare them to the things we see in our outstanding performers.

But we don't know what your people *do*.

They might be internal IT consultants. Or customer service representatives. Or regional sales managers. We don't know. And that's because this book has to serve the needs of a wide array of management-level readers.

THE WINNING CANDIDATE'S PROFILE

We're going to make an assumption. Winners possess certain qualities regardless of their specific qualities or skills. They have a core set of behaviours – habitual ways of doing things and looking at things.

- Goal orientation
- Organisation
- Initiative
- Intelligence
- Relationship-building
- Communication skills
- Leadership
- Enthusiasm
- Drive
- Resilience

- Self-development
- Stayability

We'll call this **the winner's profile.**

There are other things, of course. Things that are unique to this or that specific position. The *winner* who is an internal IT consultant will have the ability to make a computer sit up and do tricks.

Certain people are going to be successful no matter what challenge they take on because they possess a high level of these 12 core qualities which are summarised briefly in Figure 2.

And that simplifies our task as interviewers. It allows us to focus on one simple, undeniable fact.

We need to hire successful people and not just those with a successful 'attitude' or the *potential* to be successful. People who

---

1. **Goal orientation**: Has the candidate set specific and realistic goals?
2. **Organisation**: Has the candidate pursued those goals in a systematic and well-orchestrated manner?
3. **Initiative**: Has the candidate demonstrated the ability to act independently and *deal* with situations?
4. **Intelligence**: Has the candidate demonstrated the ability to solve problems and make intelligent decisions?
5. **Relationship-building**: Has the candidate built effective relationships which stand up over time?
6. **Communication skills**: Is the candidate able to get *through* to people and sell their ideas?
7. **Leadership**: Has the candidate demonstrated the ability to lead and motivate other people?
8. **Enthusiasm**: Do we see enthusiasm – especially in regard to the *goals* the candidate is pursuing?
9. **Drive**: Do we see the will to succeed – in the form of focus, determination, and tenacity?
10. **Resilience**: Is the candidate able to take problems and setbacks in their stride and learn from them?
11. **Self-development**: Does the candidate work systematically to develop their own *effectiveness*?
12. **Stayability**: Do we see the promise of a good 'fit' between the candidate and the organisation?

Fig. 2. The 12 core success qualities of a winning candidate.

have been successful in school, in previous jobs, in their hobbies, as parents.

We can give people lots of resources to work with – good products, superb training, a good territory – but we can't teach them to be successful. They have to bring that with them.

OUR CHALLENGE IN THE INTERVIEW

The key point is that certain people are going to be successful no matter what challenge they take on because they have developed or acquired certain characteristics, or habits, which are the key to success in any field.

If they can bring those characteristics into our organisation, provided they have the fundamental knowledge and skills that are needed in the specific job under consideration, they are going to be successful. Our challenge in the interview is to find out whether those characteristics are there. They provide the *target* of the interview.

And this provides us with the essential structure for the interview. Everything else – what questions to ask, what techniques to use, when to do this and when to do that – is just a means to an end.

The goal of the interview is to answer the twelve questions on the winner's profile, accurately and without having to ask them directly of the candidate.

Our goal is to answer the questions *on the basis of indirect evidence* – which means without having to resort to asking the candidate directly. If we can't do this then we call the person back in and do another interview.

So the rules are:

- You have to answer all twelve questions following the interview.

- You have to answer 'Yes' or 'No' to each of the questions. In-between or can't decide or unsure means 'no'.

- You have to do so without asking the question directly of the candidate. You have to judge for yourself, on the basis of evidence you gather about the candidate's behaviour.

Let's talk a bit about the twelve factors on the profile.

THE STARTING POINT – FACTOR 1

1. Goal orientation

The first quality is goal orientation. We need to know that the candidate has developed the habit of setting specific goals and working toward their achievement – something which is characteristic of *all* successful people.

DAY-TO-DAY EXECUTION – FACTORS 2–4

2. Organisation

We need to know that the candidate pursues their goals in an intelligent, disciplined and *effective* manner – planning ahead, thinking about what has to be done, focusing on the things that count. We need to know that the candidate works *effectively*.

3. Initiative

We need to know that the candidate is the sort of person who takes the bull by the horns and gets things done, who takes *action*, who doesn't sit around waiting for things to happen. If there is one thing that winners all have in common, it's *initiative*.

4. Intelligence

We need to know that the candidate is bright enough to think on their feet, master the challenge of learning that every new employee faces, and generally meet the intellectual requirements of the job to be done and preferably the job *after* that as well. As the business world gets more complex, as the demand for analysis and strategic thinking is pushed further and further down the corporate ladder, then the importance of the intelligence factor is heightened with every year that passes.

DEALING WITH PEOPLE – FACTORS 5–7

5. Relationship-building

We need to know that the candidate is the sort of person who builds good relationships with people, is a good team player, can bridge the gap that so often separates departments and functions, and will be an asset – simply in terms of being the sort of person who is good to have around – to you and your team as a whole.

6. Communication skills
Everyone, these days, has to be a communicator. The acid test is that they get through to people. They are able to communicate ideas and concepts. They *speak* well, and they recognise the all-important fact that communication is something that happens in the minds and hearts of the audience – not the words of the speaker.

7. Leadership
We need to know that the candidate is confident and assertive enough to move a discussion along, to make sure that certain key points are covered, to impose deadlines or standards on other people without necessarily having the 'authority' to do so, to stand up strongly in defence of an idea or proposal. The list goes on and on. There are few jobs these days in which the leadership factor does not stand the truly successful performer apart from their peers.

THE INNER PERSON – FACTORS 8–10

8. Enthusiasm
We need to know that the candidate is a positive, up-beat, en-thusiastic kind of person who enjoys their work, who gets keenly involved in things, and whose manner *communicates* their enthu-siasm to other people. It's not enough to *be* enthusiastic. It has to be a vibrant, visible quality that other people can *see* and be affected by. Winners don't keep their enthusiasm quietly to them-selves. They spread it around.

9. Drive
We need to know that the candidate is the sort of person who doesn't settle for average, who – once a goal has been set and committed to – doesn't rest until that goal has been achieved. We need to hire *outstanding* people who achieve outstanding results because they are *determined* to do so.

10. Resilience
We need to know that the candidate is someone who can rebound quickly following a setback. That's simply because results don't come quickly and they don't come without requiring that we deal with a lot of obstacles, hurdles, problems and frustrations along

the way. Winners are confident people and their self-confidence is not so fragile as to be diminished by the occasional setback.

ADDITIONAL CHARACTERISTICS – FACTORS 11–12

11. Self-development
We need to know that the candidate is someone who practices continuous learning. Good people are *always* learning, always working on their own effectiveness, always searching for ways to put their talents to optimal use and maximise the results they achieve.

12. Stayability
A winner who joins us in April and leaves at the end of August isn't going to do much 'winning' – at least not for *us*. We need to know that the candidate will stay long enough to repay the considerable investment that the company will be making in success. We can't afford to hire good people and then have them leave after only a year-and-a-half on the job.

These, then, are the 12 factors that make up the winner's profile. They are the *target* for the interview – the qualities that we are going to be looking for. Taken as a whole, they do not guarantee that a person will be outstanding but it is difficult to imagine someone being a truly outstanding performer *without* them.

4

Studying the CV

The CV gives us our first look at the candidate. And it plays a vital role in helping us whittle the initial group of candidates down to manageable size. It is sometimes one of many that we have to go through before deciding which candidates to interview.

Studying the CV is more than just a formality. It is an integral part of the selection process, and it has a number of important purposes to serve.

IDENTIFYING THE GENERAL BACKGROUND

For one thing, it is a concise and rapid way of getting the candidate's name, address, telephone number, education, job-related training, professional or industry involvements, and hobbies.

Most useful, of course, is the summary of the person's work experience: with dates, company names, job titles, and details of what was involved in each position. The CV may also indicate salary, special achievements, and reasons for leaving each job.

The CV is the first step in a series of progressively demanding hurdles the candidate must cross in order to land the job. And it is the CV which allows you to reduce a large group of candidates down to a manageable number before actually investing valuable time in interviews.

> **Don't just *read* the CV. Digest it. Take notes.**

Force yourself to generate as many hypotheses about the candidate as possible. Decide what areas of information may need to be specifically probed or explored in the interview.

Remember that it is too early to pass judgement on most candidates. What we are drawing up here are hypotheses, not conclusions. Keep that in mind as we go through the various parts of the CV and look at the information which they contain.

ASSESSING THE CANDIDATE'S WORK EXPERIENCE

Let's start with the outline of the candidate's work experience. Does the candidate have the sort of experience needed to do the job for which they are being considered?

You'll have to look beyond the mere job titles reported on the CV. Look at what specific things the candidate was *responsible* for in each position. Look at what segment of the company they worked in, who they reported to, what projects they were working on.

Look for *results*. What, specifically, has the person achieved? How significant are those achievements in light of what you know about the product or project they were dealing with.

The candidate who does not present his or her results should be suspect. There is no excuse for an outstanding candidate not telling you what he or she has accomplished.

In assessing a candidate's work experience look for people who have already done the kind of job you want them to do for you, and have done it *successfully*.

In a sales hiring situation, for example, give them one point for having any sales experience at all, another for having worked in your industry, and another for having handled a competitive or related product line. Give them a point for having handled a line that matches your own even if it is in a totally different field. Give them a point for having called on the same type of customer that your people are calling on.

And so on. That's the process we have to go through as we look at the specifics of where a person's career has taken them.

STUDYING EDUCATIONAL BACKGROUND

Look, first, at how *much* education. By and large, the key here is the presence of something beyond the secondary school level.

Then look at what *sort* of education. The ideal is probably a blend of some chemistry and biology to suggest an affinity for technical subject matter . . . and some history and literature to suggest that the candidate is a well-rounded person with broad interests.

Keep your eyes open for *too much* education, or having advanced education that has not been used in any obvious way. Be wary if the candidate has spent years taking college or university courses that are totally unrelated to the career that they have since pursued.

Look carefully, too, at the subjects taken. Do the courses tend to be in the hard, tangible disciplines or in the more abstract, theoretical ones?

The answers to these questions can tell us a lot about the candidate's motivational attributes, or about their affinity for tangible problem-solving as opposed to abstract theoreticizing.

IDENTIFYING CAREER PROGRESS

Look at what progress the candidate has made during their career. The person who has moved along rapidly might well expect to continue such movement – and this can be a positive sign of motivation, drive, and ability, or a warning of potential frustration.

Make sure that it is career *progress* you are seeing – not just movement. Look for signs of a *progressive* career. The educational part should support the subsequent work history, the work history should do justice to the education, and the career should give evidence of progression as the candidate took on increasingly challenging assignments.

If a person has had several jobs but has not made significant progress it raises a number of questions. The person may lack drive and ambition. They might be avoiding broader responsibilities or higher levels of pressure.

Note whether the candidate has spent more than five or so years in the *same* job. Companies don't usually let a really good performer linger too long in one job or at one organisational level.

But don't be too quick to judge. And, when you do, do so in the form of a *hypothesis* that will need to be tested out in the interview. Don't draw firm conclusions at this stage unless you're on a very firm footing.

LOOKING FOR CAREER STABILITY

Beware of the candidate who has changed jobs frequently, particularly if the changes have not been accompanied by visible career advancement.

It may be that the candidate works just long enough to master

a job before becoming bored with it. Or we may be looking at a decent worker but one of the first to be laid off when business slows down or the organisation trims staff.

Again, don't judge too quickly. In this era of mergers and acquisitions it's not uncommon for a good person to move through two or three different companies in quick succession.

Too much stability, of course, may indicate a lack of ambition or a reluctance to take risks. What we need to see is a judicious balance between too much hopping around and too much standing pat.

SPOTTING PORTABLE ASSETS

What tangible skills, experiences, training, insights, or product knowledge does the candidate bring with them into the job? These are what we'll call the 'portable assets'.

Generally speaking, the more portable assets there are, the less adjustment will be needed and the more immediate will be the candidate's contribution. Look carefully at what is there, and at how much of it can be transferred.

In a sales candidate, for example, the more the person knows about *who* you sell to and *how* you sell to them, the better.

If the job is in operations management look at how closely the individual's background overlaps with your own environment in terms of software, equipment, costing methods, and so on.

COMMUNICATION SKILLS

The CV is our first glimpse of the candidate as a communicator. If we were one of this person's customers or colleagues would we be impressed?

Is it an *organised* CV, for example? It should be an intelligent presentation which makes it easy for the reader to digest the basic facts at a glance. Give high marks to the candidate who gives you specific facts and verifiable numbers.

Sloppy handwriting, scratched-out errors, uneven margins, mistakes in grammar or spelling . . . or, indeed, the use of flowery language, excessively ornate or expensive paper don't make a good impression. They wouldn't impress our customers or colleagues, certainly.

We have to assume that this person will approach customers

and colleagues in exactly the same manner they have approached us.

We have to assume that what we are seeing here is how the candidate operates. Hire someone whose initial presentation is sloppy or ostentatious and you will most likely live to regret it.

INDICATIONS OF ATTITUDE

Many applicants give information which is inadvertently revealing.

For example, the candidate might write that 'I left because of a disagreement over policy' or 'I was never given a fair chance'.

Statements like these indicate an inability to adapt to the corporate environment. Their mere *presence* on the CV may suggest a certain degree of naivety.

The CV should convey a judicious blend of courtesy, professionalism, assertiveness, self-confidence, humility, and organisation of thinking. Anything that rubs you the wrong way should be cause for concern. Trust your instincts here.

INDICATIONS OF INITIATIVE

The candidate who has worked evenings in order to get through school may be more self-reliant and resourceful than one whose education was financed by others. Clues like this should not be ignored.

What we are trying to do is generate *hypotheses* based on the information we have available – hypotheses to be either validated or rejected during the interview.

THE COVERING LETTER

Look carefully at the *covering letter*. It is perhaps even more critical than the CV itself, because it ought to be addressed to our specific situation and our specific needs.

If the candidate is responding to an ad, and did *not* include a covering letter, you should be very tempted to scratch them off your list right away. Sending in a CV without a covering letter signals a basic lack of courtesy.

Think of it as a *sales* letter, with you as the prospective customer and the candidate as the 'product'.

If the letter tells you that this person is *exactly* what you are looking for, then chalk up one strike against the candidate. Without having talked to us in person, the candidate doesn't know enough about the job to make that sort of claim. If they tried that sort of thing on a real customer, it wouldn't get them very far.

If the letter is full of self-evaluations be sceptical. Good candidates usually present their achievements and let them speak for themselves. They don't *tell* you that they are creative. They are confident enough to let that fact shine through in a straightforward outline of what they have achieved.

In general, the *best* covering letter will represent a mature, down-to-earth effort to sell the idea of your inviting the candidate in for an interview. The top candidates will write a covering letter that says, in effect:

'I read your ad with great interest. It would be presumptuous to claim, on the basis of just the ad, that I am the ideal candidate – but I wouldn't be writing to you today unless I felt that the basis for a good "match" seems to be there.'

THE CANDIDATE'S FOLLOW-UP

There's another important piece of information that we have access to at this early stage – and that's what a candidate does *after* sending their CV for your attention.

Does a candidate who takes time to make a follow-up call deserve extra marks? Yes, as long as it's done professionally and maturely. Someone who makes a nuisance of themselves – and you will know the difference – deserves to *lose* a few marks. Again, trust your instincts. It's safe to assume that what you see is representative of what customers and colleagues would see if this person were to be hired.

SORTING THE CANDIDATES OUT

The CV is the first step in the selection process. Its purpose is to help us screen some candidates out and allow others to move on to the next step.

Screening a candidate means that you are deciding – on the basis of the CV – not to proceed any further. That's an important decision, and it should be made on the basis of something fairly obvious and tangible. The person has skipped around from one job to another during the past ten years, for example, or has no experience at all in our industry or with our type of customer.

How comfortable you feel making such judgements at this stage will depend largely on the *selection ratio* you have to work with. A high ratio means that there are a lot of candidates to choose from – it is a 'buyer's market' – and you have to whittle the total group of candidates down to a manageable number.

You can do it in one of two ways:

Sorting the CV's into two piles

One for those who are obviously unsuitable and one for those who warrant a closer look. Applicants in the first category can be informed of the negative decision at this stage and applicants in the second category can be invited in for interviews.

This is a good strategy to use when there is a relatively small number of candidates applying for the position.

Sorting them into three piles

This is the strategy to use when there is a relatively large number of candidates. Keep one pile for those, again, who are obviously unqualified or unsuited.

Create a second pile for those who really stimulate your interest and keep a third in-between pile for all the others.

In doing this, we have to seek a judicious balance between the need to minimise interviewing time and the need to do *enough* interviewing to ensure that we hire the best available candidate.

Each manager will have their own decision-making 'style'. Some are more cautious than others and some prefer to digest all the available data before making a final choice.

Find your own balance here. It will depend on both the prevailing selection ratio and your own decision-making style. But beware of putting too much emphasis on the CV as a screening tool. Judging people on paper is difficult, and, if we are going to err at all, it is probably best to err on the side of letting *too many* candidates get through this first critical screening test.

5

Planning the Interview

Our general strategy for the interview is to take a *behavioural* approach to the interview.

And we know what sorts of behaviour we're going to be looking for. We're going to be looking for the very same patterns of behaviour that we see in our top performers.

Now . . . let's get ready for the interview. Let's assume that you have a young lady named Heather coming in to see you at two o'clock this afternoon. What should you be doing to get ready?

PREPARING FOR THE INTERVIEW

The experienced interviewer knows that what lies ahead is something more than just a 'conversation'. A lot of information has to be gathered in a limited period of time, and the interview will be the basis for some very critical decisions. It calls for the same degree of forethought and preparation that one would apply to an important sales presentation or management meeting.

There are three important things you have to do to get ready:

- Make sure your purpose is clear.
- Review the available information.
- Plan out what you wish to cover.

ENSURING YOUR PURPOSE IS CLEAR

Many managers wander aimlessly from one topic to another during the interview simply because the objectives have been only vaguely established. The result is waste of valuable time and usually a confused or irritated candidate as well.

For *this* interview – the first – our purpose is quite clear. It's to see whether the candidate has the basic personal qualities needed to be an outstanding performer, and to decide on that basis whether to advance to a second interview.

But at other stages of the selection process, the purpose will be different. You might be probing more deeply into some troublesome points that have emerged in a previous discussion. Your goal might be to narrow things down to a short list. If you have only a single decent candidate, your purpose might be to decide whether to take a risk with that person or go back to the drawing board.

REVIEWING THE AVAILABLE INFORMATION

Long before Heather comes in to your office you should be familiar with her complete background that is available on the CV.

Or, if you are further ahead in the selection process, you will want to review the results of the testing procedure, look over the comments made by references, or read through the notes of other people who have interviewed the candidate.

By studying this you will be able to plan the interview so that as little time as possible is devoted to things which have already been covered.

PLANNING WHAT YOU WISH TO COVER

A good plan ensures an even coverage of all the areas that are important, and allows the discussion to flow smoothly from one area to another with a minimum of hesitation or awkwardness.

Before the interview begins, you should sketch out the main topics you wish to cover, determine more or less how much time should be devoted to each, and make note of any specific questions or points which need to be included along the way. Make the plan as detailed as possible, even while recognising that there will be a certain degree of flexibility in how it is executed.

DO WE NEED TO PLAN?

Do you *need* a plan? Would it not be better to allow the discussion to unfold in a spontaneous, unrehearsed fashion? Is there not a danger, if we plan the interview, of our meeting with the candidate being stilted and regimented?

Let's acknowledge that some interviewers *don't* sit down and plan things.

By and large they have become very *good* at it. They don't need to plan each and every interview because they have settled on a standard strategy which has become an intuitive part of how they conduct every interview. The plan is there but it's become part of their natural approach to interviewing.

For most of us having a plan does two important things:

- It keeps you in control of things.

- It helps us cover what has to be covered.

It keeps you in control of things

A novice interviewer tends to worry about what to talk about. In the planned interview, because there is a definite sequence of topics to be discussed, the interviewer is never in the position of having to wonder what to talk about next.

There's less rambling, fewer false starts, fewer unproductive side-journeys. Once a particular topic area has been thoroughly explored, the direction is clear and a simple 'Let's talk about . . .' is all that is required to bridge the gap.

And that helps you relax and concentrate on what is going on. The interview shouldn't be hard work.

It helps us cover what has to be covered

We can't afford to spend an hour talking about the person's education and work history and then have to rush through a cursory discussion of his or her thoughts about the future.

A plan for the interview ensures that all the relevant topic areas are explored systematically, with less danger of us giving too much emphasis to some at the expense of others – and less danger of our impressions being based on a limited sampling of the candidate's experience.

THE PLAN

There's no single best way to do this. But here's a plan that seems to work well with most people.

- Start with a bit of small talk to get the candidate feeling reasonably relaxed.

- Talk about the basic purpose of the interview and how you will do it. Make sure the basic ground rules are clear.

- Begin discussion of the candidate's background, and probably the best place to start is with their formal education.

- Move into a chronological review of the person's work history, working through to their current or most recent position.

- Talk about their career goals and aspirations – where they would like to be five or so years down the road.

- Talk specifically about why the job is attractive to them, how it fits into their career plans and how it will help them get where they want to go.

- Finally, put work-related issues aside altogether and talk about family and social life, hobbies, the *personal* side of things.

That's our *plan* for the interview. Warm-up. Ground rules. Education. Work history. Career goals and aspirations. This job and this company. Personal life and hobbies.

It's not *essential* that you do it in this order but it *is* essential that you *have* an order. There's an awful lot of ground to be covered, and having a plan is the only way to make sure it gets done.

A TIGHT SQUEEZE

Two observations. First, this is a *lot* to squeeze into an hour-and-a-half interview.

The second is, because there is so much ground to cover, we are compelled to move things along smartly and not dwell too long on any one subject. This seems to be the opposite of what we said we were going to do by taking a behavioural approach to the interview. Our goal, as you recall, is to come as close as possible to actually 'watching' the candidate at work. That means talking about who said what to whom and then what happened next. And that takes *time*.

This is why planning, and learning how to *stick* to that plan once the interview is underway, are so important.

THE FIRST OF THE TWO INTERVIEWS

This book is organised around the structure of two interviews. The first is where we do our initial screening of candidates and the second is where we take a closer look at those who have survived the initial cut.

We rarely hire a person on the basis of a single interview and there is always some degree of screening needed to get the number of finalists down to a manageable size.

Sometimes there might be two or even three 'second' interviews. Another manager might get involved or the candidate might spend some time with someone in Human Resources.

But an initial screening interview with what might be a dozen or more candidates followed by a more in-depth assessment is the usual practice.

Our goal in the first interview

Our overriding goal – the *big* goal – is to build a successful organisation. Our more *specific* goal is to hire people who will be outstanding performers and who will pay back the considerable investment that we have made in them.

Our goal in the first interview is *not* to make a final hiring decision. It is not to come away knowing that the candidate would be an outstanding sales performer. It is simply to decide whether or not the candidate deserves to be given a second interview.

6

Getting Started

We've said, in putting together our plan for the interview, that there are two preliminary tasks that have to be taken care of at the outset.

First, we need a bit of small talk to get the candidate feeling reasonably relaxed.

Second, we need to talk about what we will be trying to accomplish, and how we will do it. We need to make sure that the basic ground rules are clear.

THE WARM-UP

Our goal here is simply to get the interview off to a good start and to make sure that Heather feels good about being here. A bit of small talk is all that's needed but keep it brief and try to make it sound *real* rather than *feigned*.

'Any trouble finding us?' is one way of doing it. It's real, it's brief, and it gets the job done.

THE GROUND RULES

'Heather, I asked you to come in today because, as you know, we have a vacancy and I saw some things in your CV that suggested that an exploratory interview might be well worth while.'

This is good. You're saying something complimentary, which will further the goal of putting Heather at ease, and you're getting the basic facts of the situation out on the table.

You're also saying that this is an *exploratory* interview, and that's something that should be made clear.

'I think our goal today, Heather, should be to see whether we want to move ahead beyond this first interview. If things look good then we'll want to get together again and explore things in more depth. For today, our goal is simply to decide whether there's enough of a match here to warrant us moving ahead.'

That puts it plainly enough. Both of us have to feel good about moving ahead.

'Any questions?' is something you should add by way of bringing this portion of the interview to a close. It also gives Heather a chance to confirm that she has the same understanding of what this is all about.

THE TOOLS WE'LL BE USING

We now begin the interview proper and this will involve us talking about Heather's background: education, work history, career goals and aspirations, this job and this company, and her personal life and hobbies. That's our plan.

Encourage the candidate to talk

Our manner of conducting the interview has to be such that Heather is encouraged to talk.

Heather is probably a bit nervous and certainly anxious to make a good impression. We'll have to handle things in a manner that brings out her personality rather than causing it to be hidden behind a defensive shell.

There are three main tools we shall be using to make the interview as successful as we can.

THE LEAD-IN

The first tool is the lead-in. This takes the form of an open-ended question that we use to move into each major segment of the interview or to introduce a new subject within one segment.

'I see you've been with the Post Office for the past four years, Heather . . . could you tell me a little bit about the sort of work you've been doing?'

This is an *open-ended* question that directs the conversation into a pre-defined area without giving too much guidance as to what we are looking for. It encourages Heather to answer in whatever way she sees fit.

It's a good idea to have a specific lead-in for each major segment of the interview. That allows you to engineer a smooth transition from each one to the next.

There are two rules to keep in mind:

- First, keep the lead-in *open-ended*. Don't move into a new subject area by asking a specific question.

- Second, after asking the lead-in question, let the candidate talk. Don't interrupt.

If you open with a specific question – or if you *interrupt* by asking a specific question – you'll have to follow up with another one, and then another one after that. You, not the candidate, will carry the burden of keeping the conversation going.

You lose a valuable opportunity to see the candidate 'at work'. When you ask Heather an open-ended, unstructured question you're giving her a *problem to solve*. It's a good opportunity to see how Heather handles things:

- Did she get flustered, and ask you for more direction? Did she handle it smoothly, and display lots of poise?

- Did she stop to think a bit, and plan her overall approach, before getting started?

- Did she ramble on – to the point where you move in? Did she get bogged down in excessive detail?

THE PROBE

Our second main tool is called the probe. When we want more detail, we probe for it. This would pick up on something Heather has said – and probe for specifics. It generally starts with **what, who, when, why** or **how** and it conveys a very simple message: *Tell me more*.

- 'Did he give you a reason for his decision?'

- 'What happened when the group met again the following week?'

- 'Is that all he said?'

Probes don't have to be questions. Tell me a little bit more – if you could, Heather – about why you left. That's a probe, but it's expressed in the form of a mild directive rather than an actual question.

It's important not to be too aggressive in our probing. What did you say then? How did he react? delivered in the wrong tone can easily imply a belligerence that you may not want to have conveyed.

Show that you're getting involved, that you're eager to find out exactly what happened.

Sometimes, our probe will take the form of a *reflective statement*, one that reflects back what the candidate has said.

> 'So you felt that the meeting would be a waste of time if the CEO wasn't going to be there.'

In effect, we're asking the candidate to confirm that we have drawn the right conclusion, or to correct us if we're a bit off base.

Sometimes just a *gesture* will do. A raised eyebrow, a cocking of the head to one side, a widening of the eyes . . . any little gesture that tells the person we'd like to know more. Gestures of this sort indicate that we are *reacting* to something the candidate has said and that we want to go back and examine it.

THE FOLLOW-UP

Our third main tool is the follow-up. This is a question that we use to get at specific things that the candidate has not talked about spontaneously in response to our initial lead-in.

The follow-up is a question we insert into the discussion to fill in the blanks – when there is a specific topic that we want the candidate to talk more about.

Let's say, for example, that in talking with Heather, we moved into the area of her education. We got into it by using a general lead-in that simply asked her to talk about her educational background. Now . . . she's winding down and seems to be waiting for us to guide her into the next area but she hasn't told us which subject she enjoyed most at school, and that's something we want to know about. So, before moving on to the next area, we issue a follow-up question:

- 'Of all the subjects which you studied, Heather which one did you enjoy the most?'

- 'If you could go back and do your college years over again, is there anything you'd change or do differently?'

- 'When I started my first full-time job, I don't remember having any specific career goals in mind. How about you?'

- 'Looking back on it now, how do you feel about the way your career has unfolded? Is it the "real" you?'

Note that these follow-up questions are a bit more specific than the open-ended lead-in used to start off each segment of the interview. But they're not *too* specific. Like the lead-in, they are an invitation to talk. All we've done is narrow down the boundaries a bit.

DEVELOPING A 'MY FAVOURITES' LIST

It's a good idea to have a set of follow-up questions for each of the five main interview segments. These will be questions which you have chosen for stimulating discussion and eliciting useful information.

The important thing is that they be asked routinely in every interview. The more often you ask them, and the more answers you listen to, the more you can begin to really *interpret* what you hear.

The questions have to *sound* like you, and they have to be presented in an almost conversational fashion. Develop a list with which you feel comfortable. Have it typed up so that you can keep it in front of you when you are interviewing. Do this until they become so familiar that they flow spontaneously, with no need on your part to refer to a written guide.

You might even adapt them to suit the specific candidate you are dealing with. Some candidates respond best when you keep things businesslike and to the point. Others will react better to a more personal and conversational style. Some candidates don't mind a pointed question or a mild challenge. Others will be intimidated by it.

THE TOOLS AT WORK

Let's look at two examples of our interviewing tools at work.

Okay – we've got three tools; the lead-in, the probe, the follow-up. Let's look at how these tools work together in an interview situation. We are talking with Heather and we want to talk about the various courses and seminars she has taken.

We steer Heather into the subject by issuing a lead-in:

'I notice on your CV, Heather, that you've taken quite a few courses over the years . . .'

That's probably all we have to say. As she talks, we listen carefully and show – by the occasional nod or smile or raised eyebrow – that we are listening. And, from time to time, we use a probe to clarify a point or press for more detail:

- 'Three days seems like a lot. What was covered?'

- 'I take it, then, that every new hire went through the exact same two-week process?'

- 'You've got a course here called "Fuzzy Logic for Straight Thinkers". That sounds interesting . . .'

At some point, the conversation will wind down. Heather stops talking and waits for us to indicate where we go from here. At that point, if there are still some unanswered questions in our mind we throw out some relatively specific follow-ups:

- 'Looking back now, which of these courses do you think has had the most impact on your performance?'

- 'Are there specific things that you have been working on during the past year?'

- 'I'm curious about the course on Project Management. Is that one that you chose yourself?'

- Besides the courses that you've taken, are there other ways in which you have worked to up-grade your skills?'

DEALING WITH SETBACKS

Let's look at another example of how the **lead-in, probes**, and **follow-ups** work together in the interview situation.

We've had a good discussion with Heather and there's one last area we want to look at. How does she handle setbacks and problems? We begin with a lead-in:

'I suppose we've all had our share of setbacks, Heather. Thinking back over the past six months, what has been your biggest disappointment?'

Let's assume that she comes back with an answer that's too general to really tell us anything:

'I suppose it's the fact that I have not achieved every single target that I set out to achieve ... I tend to be quite hard on myself ...'

That doesn't tell us very much, and it seems a bit self-serving. We need to go back and repeat the Lead-in, this time elaborating a bit so that Heather knows what we're after.

'Could we take one specific target and talk about it ... a specific goal that was important to you and where you really felt disappointed when it was not achieved?'

Hopefully, that will be enough to get her on track. And, as she talks, we inject the occasional probe to clarify a point or dig for specifics:

- 'Was this a new customer, or someone you had called on before?'

- 'When the news came through that they had gone with the other firm, what was your reaction?'

- 'How exactly did you say that?'

- 'I don't quite understand why you felt he was hedging . . .'

- 'Is that something you know for a fact – or is it more of an assumption you're making?'

And we'll use occasional follow-up questions to get at specific points that we want Heather to address:

- 'Thinking now about what you were hoping to achieve, do you feel it was realistic?'

- 'What caused them to go with the competition, Heather? Why do you think it happened?'

- 'Could it have been avoided? Is there anything you could have done about it?'

- 'Looking back on it now, are there specific things that you would change about your approach?'

GOING EASY ON THE QUESTIONS

Even when the questions you are asking are unstructured ones, you should avoid asking too many. The interview should be more than a question-and-answer session. An experienced interviewer lets the candidate do the talking, and asks questions in an adroit manner that steers the flow of the conversation without intruding on it.

Specifically, if you find yourself doing more than 25% of the talking, then your manner of phrasing questions will have to be adjusted.

Too heavy a reliance on the question as a means of stimulating conversation can result in a number of problems:

1. The candidate may become defensive

When questioning is used in inquisitional fashion the results can hardly be called a 'conversation'. Even under the best of circumstances, too much questioning tends to arouse caution in the applicant. The fact that the interviewer has asked a question always implies that the subject matter is important – and the candidate can not help but tread carefully when formulating a response.

2. Less information will be forthcoming

The more questions asked, the less information is obtained. The interviewer who asks one short question after another is going to be given one short response after another. And the responses, moreover, will get shorter and shorter as the interview proceeds.

When we ask too many questions, we are saying, in effect, 'If I want to know something, I'll ask you'. And this impedes the flow of genuine conversation.

3. It places a burden on the interviewer

Once an interview has deteriorated into a question-and-answer session, it is difficult to break the pattern. The onus is clearly on the interviewer to ask the questions, and the applicant's duty is simply to respond to each one as it is presented.

Under such conditions, the interviewer has little time to think about what the candidate is saying – or even to listen carefully. They are too busy thinking about what question to ask next.

7

Examining the Five Interview Areas

Let's work through the five main areas of the interview and see if we have a winner on our hands.

There are two things going on in every interview. You and the candidate are talking about things. You're covering certain ground, spending time on certain topics. That's the *content* of the interview. You're also drawing up and testing out hypotheses about the sort of person they are and about whether they have the make-up needed to be a top performer. This is the *mental* side of the interview.

These two processes go on simultaneously. The content of the interview is divided into five main areas starting with education and proceeding through to personal life and hobbies. Your assessment of what the candidate has to offer, on the other hand, is spread across the twelve factors which make up **the winner's profile**.

Because the interview has to be organised around the five **areas** we outlined rather than the twelve **factors** we are trying to assess, it is easiest to review the **areas** first.

AREA 1: EDUCATION

Identifying educational background
We'll have a sketchy outline of Heather's educational background from the CV. Our purpose in the interview is to press for a glimpse of the person behind the education.

We begin with a **lead-in**:

'Let's talk for a while, Heather, about your educational background. I see from your CV that . . .'

and here we can add on something such as:

'You did your undergraduate work in the United States' *or*
'You went to Peterborough . . . that's where I went, too.'

The key thing is that the **lead-in** tells Heather clearly what general area we want to talk about. As she talks, we use **probes** to get at the details and **follow-ups** to get at specific aspects of Heather's educational background.

Our probes and follow-ups should be used to get at information that will help us assess Heather on the twelve dimensions that we have targeted. When we dig for information, there should be a *reason* for doing so.

Let's go through the specific factors again.

Goal orientation

'When you decided to go to college, what specific vocational plans or goals did you have in mind?'

'I'm not sure I really had a clear goal for myself when I decided to go on to graduate school. How about you?'

We ask ourselves the question: Did Heather have a specific career objective at that stage in her life, and were her educational choices made with that longer-term goal in mind?

Give high marks to the candidate whose education was consciously chosen to fit into a longer-term career plan which was realistic at the time and which has been successfully executed.

Organisation

'That was a pretty heavy workload – taking four courses and holding down a part-time job at the same time. How did you manage?'

Look for signs that Heather tackled her educational goals in a focused, systematic, disciplined manner. Probe for specifics of how she planned her work, prepared for exams, carried out major projects, and managed her time. Was she able to pace herself, tackle first things first, and get everything done?

Intelligence

'How hard did you have to work in order to get your results compared to the other students in your class?'

'How many hours per week would you say that you worked on the various subjects you were taking?'

'I see from your CV that you went into your first year at Peter- borough on an undergraduate scholarship . . .'

The sheer **content** of a person's education sometimes gives us a general measure of how much intelligence they will bring to the job. It really boils down to three critical questions:

- How difficult were the courses she took?
- How well did she do?
- How hard did she have to work?

And – has Heather made intelligent choices in regard to her education? Sometimes, a quick probe is all that's needed to dig for the information we need.

Relationship building

'During the four years you were at Peterborough, did you get involved in any extra-curricular activities?'

'Have you been able to keep in touch with either of these people during the time since you all graduated?'

We are looking for signs that Heather built friendships during her college years – friendships which have endured through to the present. Give high marks to a candidate who not only worked hard and did well but who also found time to build relationships which have stood the test of time.

Drive

'How was your education financed? Did you have to carry most of the burden yourself?'

'You had to leave Kent and head North in order to get into college . . . Was that a difficult decision?'

'Five years is a long grind. Was there any point where you got discouraged, where you felt like throwing in the towel?'

Ask yourself. Did she work her way through school? That's one question that might give us some clues. If Heather had to give up some of her leisure time it tells us something about her level of drive.

Being committed, making tough choices, making sacrifices, working hard to get where one wants to go, staying focused . . . these are all part and parcel of the drive factor.

Stayability

'Which subjects did you enjoy most while you were at Peterborough? Why was that?'

'Which subjects did you find the least enjoyable? What was there about them that you didn't enjoy?'

'Which were the subjects in which you received your best grades? Why do you think that was?'

'Which subjects did you do less well in? Why do you think that was?'

Does the candidate have a basic affinity for the products and customers she'll meet in this job? Sometimes, our discussion of the candidate's educational background can give us some clues.

If it turns out that Heather hated the 'hard' sciences, then we might have to wonder how she would enjoy working in a fundamentally *technical* area of the company. It would not be a knockout punch but it would be something to probe for at other points in the interview.

Keeping it brief

If the candidate is a recent graduate, who has little work experience, you will probably want to spend a considerable amount of time exploring their education.

With most candidates, however, you should not spend too much time reviewing their educational background. It is more instructive to look at their work experience. The personal qualities which can be assessed in our discussion of the candidate's education can be equally well and usually better assessed once we move on to the next of our five interview areas.

AREA 2: WORK HISTORY

In most cases, this will be the key segment in the interview – a chronological look at what the candidate has done during his or her career to date.

You can do it in one of two ways. One is to start with the person's current or most recent position and then work backward in time. The other way is to do it in chronological order, starting with what they did when they left school and working toward the present.

Looking at it chronologically

Here is a lead-in to get this portion of the interview started:

'What I would like to do now, Heather, is go through your career, one step at a time, looking at what was involved in each step along the way. Let's go right back to when you left school. On your CV, you indicate that you worked for two years at Post Office Counters . . .'

It's a good idea to have Heather's CV in front of you as she talks. You may also want to probe for more detail in regard to specific achievements or pieces of information which she has included.

As your discussion with Heather touches upon each of the jobs she has had during her career to date, here are the basic questions you have to keep in mind:

- How and why did she take the job?

- What was the job all about?

- What specific challenges or problems did she have to face?

- How well did she perform?

- Why did she leave?

Let's go through the specific factors which we will be looking at during this area of the interview.

Goal orientation

'I'm curious about your reasons for moving over into the marketing area . . .'

'When you went into that job, did you have any specific personal targets that you were aiming for?'

In assessing whether Heather is a goal oriented sort of person, what we look for in discussing her work history are signs that she has

- managed her career in a goal oriented fashion and

- set personal performance goals for herself in each of the jobs she has held.

Careers are shaped by the choices a person makes, and what we look for here is evidence that Heather's choices were part of game plan that she had for herself. It boils down to specifics – why she moved over into the marketing area, for example.

Organisation

'It says on your CV that you put a new telemarketing programme in place. Could you tell me a bit more about just what was involved?'

- It is always instructive to talk about how a candidate has tackled a major project. As Heather talks, probe for specifics.

- Did she start by clarifying goals and deadlines, thinking through the overall strategy, and putting together a step-by-step action plan?

- Did she use a critical path approach, with specific dates attached to each step?

- Was she realistic in her estimates of how long various things would take?

- Did she make full use of the resources around her?

- Did she get other people involved when appropriate?

- Did she consult with people who would be affected by the project or who were intended to be its beneficiaries?

Ask the unexpected
   'How do you normally plan or organise your day? Yesterday, for example . . .'

It's always revealing to ask people to talk about how they plan their day. It's one of those questions that most candidates are not expecting so you get fewer tiresome, rehearsed answers.
   It's a crucial area, too, because it gets to the heart of what good performance in *any* job is all about. Outstanding annual results or the building of long-term customer relationships are achieved *one day at a time.*
   Good performers treat time as a precious commodity that can't be wasted. They've learned to distinguish very clearly between what's important and what's not important.
   Look for evidence that Heather is allocating time in accordance with some sort of broader strategy: this percentage for telephone work, that percentage for staff meetings, and so on.
   Look for evidence that she can distinguish between what's urgent and what's important. Self-development is important . . . but it's never *urgent.* So it hardly ever actually gets put on our schedule.

> Effective performers don't just prioritise what's on their schedule; they schedule their priorities.

Initiative
If Heather has initiative, it's most likely to show up in our discussion of her work history. But we'll have to dig for it, using our probe and follow-up tools. Initiative is one of those qualities that we can assess only by looking at the details of a situation, what went through the candidate's mind and what they actually *did* and how long it took them to do it.

   'You said the meeting had to be cancelled, Heather, and you re-scheduled it for the next afternoon. Was that pretty straightforward? Around here, I mean, it's almost impossible to schedule a meeting unless you give everyone at least a week's notice . . . '

That's a probe because it follows on the heels of something that Heather has said – a seemingly innocuous statement about having to reschedule a meeting.

If we dig for the details, it might turn out that this is a glorious example of initiative. The meeting had to be cancelled and the next regularly scheduled meeting was not until the same day of the following week. But Heather decided that the meeting was critical so she spent the whole morning getting things arranged so that all of the key people except two could be there at four o'clock the next day.

That's initiative. And that's the kind of behaviour that we see day in and day out in our top performers.

Intelligence

'Tell me a bit about the up-front training you received. What exactly was involved?'

'Tell me briefly about the product, Heather. What sort of microscopes are we talking about here?'

'Okay, you got the data from the accounting people. Then what happened? Was it you who actually did the analysis?'

How difficult was the job that Heather was doing? How much learning was involved? Was it a job where she had to think quickly on her feet and decide how to handle things? Was there a lot of high-level analysis involved in her work?

We don't need to know *precisely* how intelligent she is. What's important is that we come away feeling confident that she has the solid, practical, above-average intelligence needed to do the job effectively on a day-to-day basis.

Relationship-building

'You seem to have got along well with the people in the Marketing area . . .'

'On the order desk, were calls from that same customer always routed through to the same person? Is that the way it worked?'

Look for signs that Heather has been a good team player, played an active role in committees and groups or been involved in special industry groups or professional associations. These are all signs of a <u>person who works *with* people</u> and takes <u>active steps</u> to <u>build relationships</u>.

If Heather has had order desk or customer service experience probe for signs – as we do in the question above – of her having worked closely enough with customers to build a relationship with them, even if it was only done over the telephone.

Leadership

'Was everyone in the group thinking along those same lines, or did you have to do a bit of arm-twisting?'

'You say you got the committee's approval to do a news-letter. Was that difficult? Did they have to be persuaded?'

'On those occasions when you needed the marketing re-search people involved, how did you arrange for that?'

Heather's work history is a good place to be looking for signs of leadership. Getting the boss to go along with an idea, getting the committee to give the go-ahead for a special newsletter, going to the people in marketing research and pulling them into a project . . . these are all things which might well give us a glimpse of Heather the leader in action. Or, they might not. We have to probe for the specifics.

Self-development

'What did you learn in that job? In what ways do you feel you developed during those two years?'

'You went into that job without a great deal of experience . . . What did you do to bring yourself up to speed?'

It is in our discussion of Heather's work history that we begin to look for evidence that she practices self-development. We need to look beyond the training and coursework which was built into her job and delve into what she did on her own accord to enhance her own performance potential.

We can also ask candidates to talk not so much about what they had to learn in a specific job but about what they have learned *generally* during the past year or so:

- What are some of the specific things you have been working on during the past year or two? With what results?

- How do you assess that? How do you gauge whether you've actually changed?

- In what specific ways do you feel you have changed or developed during the past year or two?

- Has that had a bearing on the results you've actually achieved in your job?

Notice, in these examples, that our follow-ups consist of a series of two or three questions rather than a single question . . . there are follow-ups to the follow-up, as it were. This is something that you'll see a lot in experienced interviewers. They ask a follow-up question, and then they ask a follow-up to the follow-up.

Stayability

'What were some of the things about that job that you especially liked or enjoyed?'

'What were some of the things that you didn't like or found distasteful?'

'What were some of the problems or frustrations you had to deal with?'

In discussing Heather's career history, we have to pay special attention to her reaction to the various jobs she has had and the companies she has worked for. This will tell us about her probable reaction to your organisation as a company to work for.

That's the question that we have tucked away in the back of our mind. **What do Heather's past reactions tell us about her future reactions?**

Not just Heather's reactions but her *choices* as well:

'You turned down Pitney Bowes and went with a small competitor. Why was that?'

'What sorts of things did you take into account in deciding to accept their offer?'

'It says here that you left in April of the following year . . .
What happened?'

Why did Heather choose this job rather than that job? What was
it about that sort of work that attracted her or led her to think it
was the right type of work for her? What is it about this type of
work that she enjoys the most?

Delve into these questions, and you'll learn a lot about the sort
of environment that brings out the best in a candidate, the sort of
people they like to work *with*.

How well did she perform?

We talked about how well Heather has actually performed in
the various jobs which she has done during the course of her
career.

One way to find out is to just ask:

'Heather, looking back on the two years you spent in the
Leeds branch, how would you assess your performance?'

Successful people focus on results and they keep track of how
they are doing. Ask them how well they performed in a job, and
what yardsticks they use to gauge that, and you will usually get a
clear, specific answer.

Here are some additional ways to get at the question of how
Heather performed:

'How would you personally evaluate your performance in
that job?'

'How was your performance in that job evaluated by other
people?'

'If you could go back and do that job over again, are there
things that you would do differently?'

Another way, of course, is to look for tangible signs of above-
average achievement – in the form of special awards, membership
in the Achievers' Club, year-end bonuses, and the like. It is
important to press for a bit of detail here. It might turn out that
the year-end bonus, or even membership in the Achievers' Club,
was pretty routine. Practically everyone got it.

And why did she leave?
How we raise this issue will depend on what we've seen on the CV.

'What were the principal reasons for your deciding to leave that job?'

'You left Barclays after only a year-and-a-half . . . How exactly did that come about?'

We sometimes get an indication of how well the candidate has performed when we find out the reasons for their leaving a job or company. This is one of those areas where it pays to do some digging rather than accepting the candidate's initial response at face value.

If she was really good, wouldn't the company have bent over backwards to try to re-locate her within another branch?

And was it really a cutback in personnel? How many people were let go, for example? Were they replaced? Were they all let go at the same point in time – or was this clearly an individual termination?

But tread carefully here. Don't *assume* there's some sort of hidden reason for her job being terminated. Try not to be a cynic. But – if you have to choose between being a cynic who assumes that there is *always* a reason for someone being let go, and being someone who naively accepts things at face value and assumes that the person is telling the whole story . . . by all means be a cynic.

AREA 3: CAREER GOALS AND ASPIRATIONS

Where is the candidate going – and why? This third area of the interview looks at what lies ahead in the candidate's career.

There are two ways of looking at this. The first is to address the issue of specific career goals and objectives and to talk about what Heather is looking for at this point in her career.

The other is to talk more generally about the ideal job, the ideal boss, the ideal environment. If Heather does not have specific career goals, she still ought to be able to talk coherently about what sort of job, what sort of boss, and what sort of work environment tend to bring out the best in her.

Let's start with the more specific issue of career goals and objectives. The lead-in:

> 'Let's look now – if we could, Heather – at what you see lying ahead in your career and where you'd like to be five or so years down the road.'

Then we let Heather talk, and we listen.

One important note – don't be swayed too much by the candidate's outward *style* as they talk about this area. An experienced candidate will recognise the need to talk about career goals and aspirations, and will have put some thoughts together. A less experienced candidate may have to stop and think a bit. That doesn't necessarily mean that aspirations are any less real. It *might*. But it might not.

Goal orientation

> 'Where do you see yourself going from here? Where would you like to be five years from now, for example?'

> 'Are there other options that you're looking at, or have you pretty well made up your mind about things?'

> 'How did you set those goals? Did you actually sit down and think about them, and write them down?'

What we want to see are signs that Heather has clear and specific goals for her career – that she knows exactly where she is going.

If she seems unclear or gives an answer that is rather general we may want to use a follow-up:

> 'Are there specific yardsticks or benchmarks that you would use to assess how your career is going? For some people, for example, it's how much money they're making. Or being the number one performer on the team . . .'

Successful performers tend to have specific goals. They know quite precisely where they are going and how they will know when they have arrived. If Heather seems vague about her goals, press for some specifics. If she has difficulty being more specific, stop pressing. If you press too hard, there's a good chance that she'll invent some goals right there on the spot because you're so obviously looking for them.

Are Heather's goals realistic? Could it be said that Heather is shooting too *low* – that her goals aren't challenging *enough*?

Stayability

'What are the things that are important to you in a job or in a company? Why?'

'What are some of the things you would wish to avoid in a job or in a company?'

'How would you describe the ideal boss? What sort of manager really brings out the best in you?'

Heather's answers to these follow-ups may give us some important clues regarding the stayability factor. Is what she is looking for compatible with what she is likely to get? Can we satisfy her needs? Are her goals realistically achieveable within the time frame that she has in mind?

The basic question is this. Is what we're hearing from Heather consistent with what we know about the job for which she is being considered? How close is the overlap between what Heather considers ideal and what she is likely to experience if she joins us?

AREA 4: THIS SPECIFIC OPPORTUNITY

In this area we talk about this specific opportunity. What are the person's thoughts about the role for which they are a candidate? And what are his or her thoughts about your company or organisation as an employer?

'I'd like to talk now, Heather, about your view of this particular opportunity. To start, do you have any basic questions about the job?'

At some point in the interview, we have to give Heather an opportunity to ask questions about the job, and now is probably a good time to do it. Remember what we said about hiring being a two-way street . . . both sides have an important decision to make.

Then, we ask *our* questions.

Self-development

'If you join us, obviously, you'll be dealing with a whole new kind of customer . . . what sort of adjustments do you think might be needed on your part?'

'One of my concerns is that you haven't dealt with this complex a product before. Any thoughts about that?'

'Is there anything special that you've done to get ready for this new assignment?'

There will be some sort of learning curve. There always is, even when a person is making a sideways move rather than joining the organisation for the first time. So we ask whether Heather accurately recognises the slope and duration of the learning curve and has she done a thorough assessment of the 'fit' between her own skills and the demands of the role.

Stayability

'From where you stand, what do you see as the main challenges or difficulties in this job?'

'I've talked about some of the challenges we're facing out in the field and some of the new directions we're taking . . . how do you see yourself making a contribution?'

'Have you talked to your partner about this opportunity? How do they feel about it?'

'What appeals to you in this job that you have not had in your previous situation?'

This is an absolutely crucial area because a hiring decision has to work both ways. It has to give us the very best person for the job but it also has to give the candidate what they are looking for and what they *need*. It has to be a mutual decision.

It is worth noting that what a candidate is looking for and what they need are not always the same thing. A candidate might want the job badly and see it as a logical next step in their career and be excited about being part of your organisation. But if they need a lot of direction, or need to be able to work at a relaxed pace and not have too many balls up in the air at one time then they are not going to be successful in this job or in this company.

And people don't always *know* what they need. It's part of our job to find these things out and take whatever course of action we feel is best for both sides. If the person's needs are not going to be met, no matter how badly they want the job or how enthusiastic they are, we owe it to both them and us to steer them away.

Comparing this to the ideal
It is often helpful to link the discussion of the ideal situation – in the Career Goals portion of the interview – to the discussion of this specific opportunity. For example:

Under Career Goals we asked:

'Ignoring this particular opportunity for a minute, what are the specific things you're looking for at this stage in your career?'

'Anything else?'

And now, under This Opportunity, we follow up with:

'You've talked a while ago about some of the things you're looking for at this stage in your career . . . Do you think you'll find them here?'

Under Career Goals we asked:

'Ignoring this particular opportunity, if you had to pick one company to work for, who would it be? Why is that?'

And now, under This Opportunity, we follow up with:

'A little while ago, you said that somewhere like ASDA or Tesco might be a good place to work . . . How would you think this company might compare to ASDA?'

Under Career Goals we asked . . .

'How would you describe the ideal boss? What sort of manager really brings out the best in you?'

And now, under This Opportunity, we follow up with:

'You described your ideal boss a bit earlier. What's your sense about the kind of boss you might have if you got this job?'

AREA 5: PERSONAL LIFE AND HOBBIES

There's a lot to talk about here – current family situation, social activities, leisure-time pursuits, hobbies, general 'lifestyle' – but the discussion needn't be time-consuming. Try to zero in on the things that really tell you something meaningful about Heather the person.

Goal orientation

We look for signs that Heather has set goals for herself in regard to her hobbies. Not *all* of them. A lot of what a person does in their leisure time ought to be done for the sheer pleasure of doing it. Still, most people will have one, perhaps two hobbies in which the idea of setting specific goals is quite relevant.

If it turns out that Heather would like to learn a foreign language . . . does she, or *has* she, set goals? Are those goals specific? Are there target dates attached? Are the goals realistic and achieveable? Are they *challenging* goals?

Organisation

'I see on your CV that you founded a Girl Guides chapter. That sounds like quite an achievement. Could you tell me a bit more about it?'

'When you took the year off to travel to the Orient, what sort of planning went into it?'

It is always helpful to talk with candidates about how they *planned* something. When people talk about how they did it you'll get a glimpse of how they set goals. You'll see whether they established an overall strategy and translated that strategy into a coherent action plan. You'll see whether their plan was based on an accurate estimate of how long things would take or how much things would cost.

Relationship-building

One of the things to look for in discussing a candidate's background during this first interview is evidence of *sociability*. Are

Heather's hobbies solitary or do they being her into contact with other people? Does she belong to any clubs? Is she active in the community? Does she seem to watch a lot of television?

Drive

'You mentioned music as being one of your hobbies . . . could you tell me a bit more about that?'

As we talk to Heather about her hobbies and leisure activities, we should be looking for signs that there is a competitive colouring to the things she enjoys the most – and that it is this competitive element, in fact, which makes these things enjoyable.

How intensely is Heather involved in her major hobby? Does she do something for a couple of months and then get bored with it, or has her hobby been a lifelong pursuit? Is it perhaps taken *too* seriously? If it's taken very seriously, what does she do for *fun*?

Stayability

'I see under hobbies, on your resumé, you've put "Hell's Angels" . . . I take it that's a club or community group of some sort . . .'

In talking about the candidate's family and social life ask yourself – Is this *our* kind of person? We ask this question with some trepidation, but it's an important one. Someone who hangs out with motorcycle gangs may not be quite this company's cup of tea. It's difficult to know just how to judge such things, and it's obviously important that you put your own *personal* biases well into the background, but the question does have to be raised on occasions. Your intuition will generally tell you when it's appropriate.

A balanced lifestyle

Look for signs of a balanced lifestyle. Winners, most often, are people who both work hard and play hard. They attach importance to leisure time, and they don't waste it.

Ask what the candidate does with their leisure time. Is there evidence that they plan ahead? That they have personal goals? Do they want to learn to play the piano? Do they have a pretty clear idea of how much time they want to spend with the family every week?

Do they take good care of themselves? Do they engage in exercise and athletics? Do they consciously acknowledge the importance of being fit and healthy insofar as being a productive on-the-job performer is concerned?

8

Examining Strengths and Weaknesses

Through our discussion of Heather's work history, and to a lesser extent her education and career goals, we are able to draw up an accurate view of her strengths and weaknesses . . . to the point where it may not be necessary to devote a specific chunk of the interview to discussing them.

It is also a deceptive area for someone who doesn't interview people often to be delving into. Candidates expect to be asked about their strengths and weaknesses, and most will have taken time to formulate some answers, so it is difficult to know just how much stock to put in what you hear.

Still, let's insert it in between the work history and career goals of the first interview – the rationale being that this seems to be the spot which would allow the interview to flow most naturally.

STARTING WITH STRENGTHS

Because this area can be a bit threatening for some candidates, it's best to ask about strengths first and then shortcomings afterwards.

Try to move into the subject in a natural way that flows from the preceding discussion without explicitly attaching the 'strengths and weaknesses' label to the topic.

> 'We've talked about some of the things you've achieved over the past five years, Heather . . . and you seem to have done quite well for yourself. What are some of the specific things about you that you feel have accounted for the success you've had?'

Some candidates will have difficulty getting started on this question, and you might have to follow up with a gentle prod.

> 'Here's the type of thing I mean. I have a daughter at home who's really inquisitive – to the point where it drives me

crazy at times. But I know that's always going to be one of her real strengths, and I want to encourage it.'

If you only get one or two statements from the candidate, you can encourage them to continue simply by asking, 'Is there anything else you can think of?'

Being prepared to probe

In discussing a candidate's strengths, you should be prepared to probe a bit.

Most importantly, find out *why* something, in the candidate's view, is a strength. Here are some examples.

'What would you say there is about you that has accounted for your career progress to date?'

'How exactly has that "accounted for your career progress" . . . ?'

'What would you say are your main strengths? Areas where you are distinctly above-average?'

'This probably sounds like an odd question, but . . . how do you know that? How do you know you're above-average in that area?'

These are powerful one-two combinations. A follow-up question which puts the issue on the table and then a probe which asks the candidate to go back and elaborate on their initial response.

With some candidates, you may wish to issue a mild challenge if you don't agree with their view of their own strengths and weaknesses:

'You've mentioned assertiveness as being one of your strengths. I'll be quite honest with you – it's one of the things I've been a bit concerned about . . .'

Why should I hire you?

It's old and it's corny, but it's still a very powerful question to ask at this stage in the interview:

'I know this sounds like a corny question, but . . . why should I hire you? Seriously. Give me your best sales pitch!'

MOVING ON TO WEAKNESSES

Do it in a natural, conversational way that flows easily.

> 'How about the other side of the coin, Heather? Anything about you that you feel could be strengthened?'

> 'What are the things you feel less confident about . . . things that you'd like to improve?'

> 'How do you assess that? How do you gauge whether you've actually changed?'

> 'Has that had a bearing on the results you've actually achieved in your job?'

Again, don't end this area of the discussion too soon. This is where a wee bit of pressure is quite acceptable . . . Anything else you can think of, Heather?

Dealing with virtues-in-disguise

Most candidates realise that they are going to be asked about their shortcomings and they recognise that it's not good to simply state that they don't have any. Most often they'll start with a few innocuous items which might even be considered virtues.

> 'I suppose my biggest weakness is that I expect too much from myself.'

> 'I know I sometimes get impatient with people who are content to go through the motions or who expect me to do their thinking for them.'

> 'I don't suffer fools gladly. It's a bad trait, I know, and my wife gets after me about it.'

> 'I'm not much of a "politician", I suppose. I tend to call it the way I see it, and that's gotten me into hot water a few times.'

This is the sort of self-congratulatory stuff you get from a sophisticated candidate. They are 'confessing' to weaknesses which we all know are really signs of strength.

Put up with it. Let the person talk. Don't get your back up. Wait your turn. And then come back with something like:

'Well, okay. But I can see how being too tough on people might also be considered a strength, depending on how you look at it. Is there anything that's really a shortcoming . . . something that you know prevents you from achieving the sort of results that you would otherwise be capable of achieving?'

Let the candidate know, without being offensive or cute about it, that you can see through their ruse. Explain how you define a 'shortcoming' then wait for an answer.

A USEFUL ONE-TWO COMBINATION

A good way to get at strengths and then weaknesses is to ask the candidate to look ahead in time . . . to hypothesise:

'Let's imagine you join us, and you've been here a year, and you've achieved outstanding results . . . what are the most likely reasons for that happening?'

'Let's imagine, heaven forbid, that you've been here a year and we both decide that it's not working out . . . what are the most likely reasons for that happening?'

SELF-DEVELOPMENT

Your discussion with Heather about how she views her own strengths and weaknesses is an excellent time to zero in on the self-development factor.

'If these are your strengths, Heather, in what way have you worked to develop and fine-tune them over the years?' And, 'If these are your weaknesses, what are you doing about them?' We don't say it in those words, but that is the essence of what we talk about.

'You talked about your enthusiasm as being a strength – Does that come naturally, or is it something you have to work at?'

'You've said that you'd like to know more about the Marketing side of things. Have you taken any concrete steps to do that?'

'You mentioned your tendency to take on too many things at one time . . . Is there something you've tried to do about that?'

USING A QUESTIONNAIRE

Because asking people about their strengths and weaknesses is such an obvious thing it might be better to come at it from a different angle.

Let's give Heather a list of 30 relevant strengths and ask her to earmark the five where she feels she is strongest and the five where she feels she is least strong. Then the next five strongest and the next weakest. In effect, what we are doing is creating a frequency distribution which forces Heather to make choices.

Then, rather than asking her to talk about her strengths and weaknesses, we can take a copy of her questionnaire and run through the results together.

'You indicate, Heather, that "multi-tasking" is one of your strengths. Do you think you could expand a bit on what that term means to you?'

9

Listening to What's Being Said

In this chapter, we're going to look more closely at the listening side of how the effective interviewer goes about their business.

- We shall examine what is involved in *effective listening*.

- We'll look at the *reflective response*, a good way to let the candidate know that you're listening, and to carry your understanding further.

- We'll look at the task of *dealing with silence* and see why it should be welcomed, not kept at bay.

EFFECTIVE LISTENING

Good listening is one of the essential foundation stones of the effective interview. A good interviewer knows that careful listening requires a lot of mental discipline. There is a lot to do during the interview. You have to guide the conversation, ask pertinent questions, write down whatever notes you feel are necessary, and keep an eye on the time . . . and these various duties can easily interfere with your concentration.

Let's look, then, at a few essential and very helpful guidelines.

- Make sure you are well prepared.

- Take steps to prevent interruptions.

- Give the candidate your full interest.

- Do things that show that you're interested.

Make sure you are well prepared
Before sitting down with the candidate, you should have:

- done a thorough review of all the available information

- taken time to think through what lies ahead and develop a rough plan for the interview

- taken steps to ensure that any documentation you might wish to refer to during the interview is close at hand.

Take steps to prevent interruptions

The interview cannot proceed smoothly if the telephone is ringing, or if someone is knocking on your door, or if there is a loud and very audible discussion being held in the next office.

Take active steps to ensure that there will be no distractions or interruptions while the interview is taking place.

Give the candidate your full interest

This may sound very basic, but it is surprising how many people try to conduct an interview while their minds are preoccupied with other matters. It may be a specific issue that you were wrestling with that morning, or a meeting to be held later that day. Regardless of what it is, either put it out of your mind or else stop the interview and take care of it.

Do things that show that you're interested

Nod your head occasionally. Smile when the candidate says something humorous. Use phrases such as 'That's interesting' and 'I see' to signal your interest in what's being said.

The important thing is not to sit there passively. You have to show that you're listening intently and are interested.

THE REFLECTIVE RESPONSE

A good listener doesn't just passively absorb what the other person is saying. They take active steps to encourage the other person to talk.

The use of the reflective response is an excellent way to let the candidate know that you are really listening and that you are making a genuine effort to understand its meaning.

Try, in fact, to go beyond what the candidate has said. Try to go a bit beyond where the candidate left off.

Let's look at an example, and then examine why such a technique is so useful a tool.

> 'You said earlier, Heather, that Jackie was one of the best supervisors you've ever had. What was it about her that you especially liked?'

> 'With Jackie, you knew what was expected. There was no waffling. You knew what had to be done and you knew when it had to be done by.'

> 'You like someone who provides pretty clear direction, and Jackie was that kind of person.'

> 'Yes. I've never really liked a boss who says "Well, you just go ahead and do it whatever way you feel is best . . .".'

> 'Anything else about Jackie that you especially liked?'

The value of the reflective response is that it does not threaten the candidate or impede the flow of conversation.

You are simply showing the candidate that you are interested in what is being said and that you are making a genuine attempt to understand it.

You are also giving the candidate a chance to correct you if your understanding is wrong or slightly off track.

Let's look at an example of how this can happen.

> 'What were the reasons for your deciding to leave the company at that stage in your career?'

> 'I wasn't really too happy with the way things were going, to be honest with you, and I really felt that a move at that stage would be the best thing for both me and the company.'

> 'It sounds, then, like you and the company weren't getting along too well – and that leaving just seemed the best thing to do.'

> 'It's not so much that we weren't getting along. The problem was really that I had stopped growing in my job. There just wasn't anything more to look forward to, and both I and the company knew it.'

It's not a bad idea to sometimes deliberately mis-state what the candidate has told you. This is particularly helpful if you feel they avoided answering a question, or have given you only a partial or one-sided answer.

In effect, you're challenging them to come right back and correct you. And, by doing so, to go a bit further than they did the first time around.

FEELING THE FACTS

Among the 'facts' we're interested in are things like emotions and interpretations. This is where the reflective response is so useful. It helps to pin down the emotional or cognitive events that transpired. And they are every bit as important as behavioural events.

Feelings represent the candidate's reactions to facts and events. As such, they are an important source of information. They can often be elicited by a brief, direct question. 'How did you feel about that?' or 'I guess that came as a bit of a blow, didn't it?'

It is important that you take the lead in soliciting these reactions. Most candidates, left to their own devices, will tend to stick to the facts. So you have to let them know, by the questions you ask, that you're interested in subjective and emotional facts as well.

DEALING WITH SILENCE

Most people feel uncomfortable when there is a noticeable pause in a conversation. There is a distinct pressure there to say something.

The novice interviewer often jumps in quickly to repeat the question or ask a new one. The experienced interviewer has learned to use it to their advantage as a very valuable interviewing technique.

Silence asks, without the use of words, 'What else can you add?' It is an invitation to continue.

Good interviewing

The acid test of good interviewing is the **completeness** with which the candidate discusses things. If you want them to give you the full story, you have to allow enough time to do so. Once you have asked a question, assume that the candidate knows that it is their turn to speak. If a response is not immediately forthcoming, resist the temptation to jump in and repeat the question, add to it, or answer it yourself. Give the candidate a proper chance to respond.

Give the process a fair chance to proceed at its own pace. The information that emerges after a period of silence is often far more meaningful than that which springs from a fast-moving, non-stop discussion.

SOME ADDITIONAL GUIDELINES

The truly effective interviewer has acquired the knack of making the whole thing seem like a relaxed, casual conversation still keeping the basic objectives in mind and gearing everything toward their achievement. There is a fair amount of 'technique' involved with this and it's worth covering them now:

- Listen for the meaning of what is said.

- Use questions to maintain concentration.

- Be alert to how things are being said.

- Be yourself. Be as natural as you can.

Listening for the meaning of what is said.
If the candidate uses a word or phrase which can obviously have more than one meaning – take time to verify your interpretation.

Ask them to clarify what was meant. Or repeat back your own interpretation of what was said, and ask the candidate if that was what they intended.

Using questions to maintain concentration
There is a limit to our capacity for concentration – and it will vary from one interviewer to another.

If you find your attention straying from what the candidate is saying, it may be helpful to wait for an appropriate moment and then ask a question. This is a good way of staying 'tuned in' to the discussion.

Being alert to how things are being said

Keep a watchful eye on vocal mannerisms, inflection, gestures, facial expressions, and body posture. These can be valuable clues to what the candidate is actually thinking and feeling.

Look for discrepancies between what is being said and **how** it is being said – and don't be afraid to point out your observations in a natural and constructive fashion.

> 'You've said you're excited about the job, Heather. But I've got to be honest with you . . . you don't *look* excited.'

Then stop. The candidate will know that you expect them to resolve it for you. You don't have to say anything else.

Being as natural as you can

Don't over-do eye contact and don't over-use the various tools that we have been talking about.

Be yourself. If you're in the habit of chewing on the end of a pencil, or twirling your glasses, then do it so long as you are listening to what the candidate is saying and making a genuine effort to understand.

But use common sense. If your habit is that of drumming your fingers on your desk then an effort to break it would obviously be well advised.

MAINTAINING A POSITIVE ATTITUDE

Throughout the interview, it is important to maintain a positive attitude. The candidate should go away thinking that they have made a positive impression. We shouldn't even mind if twelve different candidates go away thinking they've got the job!

If you think you're making a good impression, you relax and you begin to see the real candidate. They begin to lower their guard.

If the person hints that the main reason they were not promoted into a managerial role is because they have a boss who's been holding them back . . . play on it. Nod your head knowingly and say that, yes, that's not an uncommon story . . . you've seen it happen all too many times before. Shake your head slowly. Why, it's a damned shame when that kind of thing happens. It's not fair.

It encourages the candidate to continue. You can tell by the tone of their voice that what's coming out now is real.

Playing down unfavourable information

When the candidate says something that is awkward or difficult to admit, it's usually something you want to hear more about.

If you ask a direct question about the issue you're likely to cause the candidate to start cautiously filtering out what they say.

Play the point down. Say that what they have just told you is a common experience that happens to the best of us. If they say that they failed a specific course at college and had to repeat it the next year you might say 'Well, I never had any problems with physics when I was at school, but I bombed out in history. What was it about the physics course that you had trouble with?'

Let the candidate know that there's nothing terrible about what it is they've admitted to. In fact, you're interested. You'd like to hear more.

Avoiding disagreement

Once in a while, a candidate might say something that will make you want to argue the point.

The interview is not the time or the place for you to signal disapproval or disagreement. That is not to suggest that you have to pretend to approve of something that you don't approve of. All we are saying is that you shouldn't react.

Say something non-judgmental that helps keep the conversation going.

Using positive reinforcement

One of the things you can do to create a non-judgmental climate in the interview is to pay the candidate a compliment.

If the candidate tells you that they worked five evenings a week to help finance their education you might say: 'I like that. It's the kind of thing I'm hoping my kids will do when the time comes'.

Be sincere. Anything that smacks of insincerity will work *against* the creation of the right climate, not in favour of it.

Every candidate will have something that deserves a word of praise and there's no better way of getting them to talk spontaneously than to give a simple and genuine compliment when it is suitable.

10

Digging For Behavioural Gold

We want to draw as detailed and realistic a picture of the candidate's past performance as we possibly can. And we have to do it through the candidate's own story-telling.

It's human nature to recall the good things and forget the bad, particularly when the story-teller is also the chief character in his or her own story, so our task is to get at the 'facts' of what actually happened.

THE BEHAVIOURAL DIG

The behavioural dig – as opposed to an *archaeological* dig – involves taking a specific incident and delving into it deeply. For example:

'I'm still not sure I understand, Heather, why Jack was balking at letting you go ahead with the project. The cost didn't seem to be out of line . . .'

'I think it was more a question of Jack being a bit apprehensive about the fallout over in Consumer Products.'

'How do you mean – "fallout"?'

'We'd been getting the lion's share of the new product funding since I took over Industrial and Bill Parnell moved to Consumer, and I think Bill felt it was getting time to even up the score a bit.'

'Why would that make Jack apprehensive? I'm still not sure about this word "fallout".'

'I think Bill had been putting some pressure on Jack to move more funding over to the Consumer side.'

'From the way you described Jack earlier, he doesn't sound like the sort of person who would succumb to pressure from one of his underlings.'

WHEN TO STOP AND DIG

But we can't do it for everything. There just isn't time. So we have to choose our time carefully and dig under the surface to get the information we need.

Here are some of the conditions under which the behavioural dig should be used:

- When the candidate has been reviewing their background in such broad, general terms that you haven't really been learning anything.

- When you sense that the candidate has been describing things in a manner designed to put themself in the most favourable light.

- When the incident or situation being discussed is similar to situations that the candidate would encounter if hired into the new job.

- When the situation is one that you yourself have had first-hand experience with, or which is simply of great interest to you.

LEAD-IN . . . THEN PROBE, PROBE, PROBE

The structure of a behavioural dig starts with a lead-in and follows up quickly with a series of pointed probes.

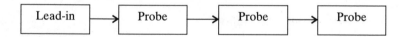

The lead-in gives the candidate a scenario to work with then we use our probes to go after the details we think will be useful. It is clearly you, the interviewer, not the candidate, who is in charge of the ship.

For example:

'As a sales rep, Heather, do you find that you sometimes have to lock horns with head office in order to get approval for something special that you want to put together for a customer? Can you give me an example?'

That's the lead-in. Heather will talk for a while, but probably not in enough detail to satisfy our need to be a 'fly on the wall'. So we'll have the following probes waiting in the wings:

- Who was the customer?

- What was it that you were trying to do?

- I take it, then, that that sort of thing required head office approval?

- What was the reasoning behind the package you were trying to put together?

- Was there a strategy or a plan in your mind when you approached head office?

- Who did you talk to? By telephone?

- What was his (her) initial reaction?

- How exactly did he (she) express that to you?

- What did you do or say at that point?

- Then what happened?

UN-QUESTIONS: THE PROD

Most candidates are anxious to make a good impression, and all but the most inexperienced will have developed certain stock answers that they've used again and again.

When you start digging for behaviour, though, it may catch the candidate off-guard. You may find that a candidate – now that they can see that you aren't going to be taken in by a lot of generalities – resists your efforts to probe for specifics.

We want to get over this hurdle without over-relying on the *question* – remember what we said about going easy on the questions. So we use something that we'll call the 'un-question'. It comes in four different forms:

1. The calculated pause

It's early on in your interview with Heather and you've just asked her to tell you what was the most challenging aspect of her last job. And her answer is . . . total silence.

It's tempting to jump in and say something, just to break the silence, and move on to something else.

The best advice is not to rush. Use what might best be called a calculated pause. Just wait – ten seconds doesn't sound like a long time but in an interview it can seem like an eternity.

It might be that Heather just needs a little time to sort out what's important and what's not. Remember – the sort of interviewing we're doing is aimed at getting the candidate to **think**. So we need to give her plenty of time to do that. Don't rush.

2. A 'That's Okay' statement

Heather still hasn't said anything and the silence has gone on now for a good fifteen seconds. What started as a calculated pause is fast becoming an awkward pause. What do we do now?

Don't panic. Let's break the silence without letting Heather off the hook by skipping on to the next question. Instead, use what might best be thought of as a 'That's Okay' statement.

'I know it's sometimes a bit difficult to think back and remember precisely what happened. When I ask people a question like that, it often takes them a moment or two – but that's okay because I learn a lot when we look at exactly what happened.'

What the 'That's Okay' statement does is tell the candidate that it's okay to not have a quick answer. It happens to most people. Relax, don't worry about it. Don't get self-conscious.

This is important, because you want the candidate to talk freely and explore things spontaneously.

Make sure you smile sympathetically when you issue a 'That's Okay' statement. Your words and your manner have to be 'in synch'. If you glance at your watch or let a tone of irritation creep into your voice, nothing you can say will prevent the candidate from tightening up even more.

3. Restatement

Heather still hasn't said anything. By now it's quite clear that she's at a loss for words and something more than a 'That's Okay' statement is needed to un-freeze her.

Our next technique is a simple restatement of the question. Don't repeat it word for word. If you do that, you're *bound* to let a hint of impatience creep into your voice.

Change the wording slightly. Shift the emphasis a bit:

> 'What I'm looking for, Heather, is an example from your last job of something that really put you to the test – a problem or a situation that was a real challenge for you . . . Can you recall something like that?'

4. Polite persistence

Sometimes a candidate will state quite proudly that one of their strengths is they aren't afraid to challenge the status quo. That's good, because you want the candidate to be innovative and being innovative is going to require that the person will not be afraid to challenge some long-standing practices and assumptions.

Still, we need to see some evidence:

> 'Can you think of a specific example of your challenging the status quo? Can you give a specific example from the past couple of months?'

And he says:

> 'Well, it's something I do a lot of. It's just part of the way I approach things. If it means challenging the status quo, I'm not afraid to do it.'

Here, the candidate seems to be trying to dodge the question, and your task is to point out as politely as you can that evasion just isn't going to work.

Polite persistence is the order of the day:

> 'I realise it's a bit difficult to come up with specific examples but can you think of a recent situation where you challenged the status quo?'

SUMMARY

The behavioural dig, then, involves taking a particular event and delving into it until genuine understanding has been achieved. It involves probing. Trying to re-create what actually happened.

The advantage of doing this is that it gives you a chance to 'observe' the candidate at work. It gives you a 'feel' for how the candidate approaches things, and what strategies they use in pursuit of an objective.

QUESTIONS AND ANSWERS

Generalities versus specifics

If you ask someone a general question – 'How do you go about organising projects?' – you're likely to get a general answer.

Then you're left with the issue of whether you can trust what they're telling you. Maybe they don't know how they organise projects? Maybe they're just saying what seems logical, or what they think they're *supposed* to say.

It's better – much better – to ask the person how they organised the *ABC* project, or the *XYZ* project.

One reason why this is good is that no one has probably asked them how they organised that specific project before.

That leads to reason number two. Because they haven't had to think about this before, you'll be able to watch them as they actually think through a problem. It's a glorious opportunity to actually see them in action, first-hand.

And the third reason is that it comes closest to being a fly on the wall and actually watch them as they talk through the organisation of a specific project.

Behaviour versus outcomes

The main reason for digging for behaviour is because that is where we see the patterns that tell us what kind of person the candidate is. And it's by understanding what kind of person the candidate is that we are able to predict the future.

Let's clarify some terms here:

- Behaviour: This is what actually happens. Jim says this. Jack does that. Bill reacts this way. Harry handles the meeting that way.

- Outcomes: These are the results of that behaviour. Sales increased. Three people left. Candidate got promoted.

- Environment: And all this took place in a particular environment. Behaviour produced outcomes under this or that set of conditions.

We see a lot of the outcomes information on the resumé and we'll hear a lot of it during the interview.

The person tells us that he or she opened twelve new accounts over a two-year period.

Can they do the same sort of thing for us? That's the real question. We're intelligent enough to know that the environment here isn't the same as the environment there.

But what we don't do enough of is go back and look at the behaviour that produced those outcomes.

How did they manage to open twelve new accounts over that two-year period? Take any one of them and ask how they acquired that particular account. If it hinged on two or three crucial meetings with the prospective customer, take one of them and ask how they handled it. Within that meeting, how did they handle this or that particular objection, or present this or that particular point?

We have to predict what sort of behaviour we're going to be getting and what outcomes that behaviour is likely to produce in our unique environment.

Personality and patterns
When we look at it this way, it reinforces the idea that the concept of personality is nothing more than a shorthand way of describing certain patterns of behaviour that the person will be bringing into the new job in the new environment.

It's those patterns that we're really hiring, not the actual behaviour – that's gone. But if we don't see the behaviour, we won't see the patterns.

We'll know what outcomes the person was able to produce in this or that previous environment and, as far as we can, that's predicting the future.

11

Probing for Specifics

We are going to tailor our questioning of the candidate to the specific demands of the job for which they are being considered. For example:

1. Internal consulting skills
2. Project management
3. Attention to detail
4. Customer relationships
5. Management style
6. People development

We'll use the behavioural dig – our potent combination of a scenario-setting lead-in followed by a series of sharp probes – to get the candidate to resurrect an example of a specific competency in action.

> 'Tell me, Heather, about a situation where you had to exercise leadership.'

Some general points.

- We're probing for behavioural specifics. The more we get at actual behaviour, the more we learn about how the candidate actually performs.

- Our questions start out being quite broad and unstructured as we lead the candidate into the area. Then we begin to narrow them down and make them more structured.

- We try to probe for positive things first. We do not want this to be a cross-examination or an inquisition. Then we shift our focus to the less complimentary side of things.

- We won't always ask the same questions in the same order. We still want the conversation to flow as naturally as possible.

- Some of the questions might not even have to be asked at all if the information we are after is volunteered. The questions are just tools to be used when and if we need them.

INTERNAL CONSULTING SKILLS

'I know an important part of your job is the quality of the relationships you are able to establish and maintain with end-users. What are some of your strengths in this area?'

That's the general lead-in. It guides the candidate into the area we want to talk about; then we get down to specifics:

'Sometimes a client comes to us for help and isn't quite sure what they want. Can you think of an example of this happening to you?'

- What was the situation?

- How did the client approach you? What did they say?

- What did you say then?

- Is this how you would normally handle that type of situation?

- Can you think of another example?

In the above example, we're looking for how a systems person helps an end-user define their needs. It's a very important part of what makes an internal consultant successful.

'Tell me about the most frustrating experience you've had, trying to help a client or end-user solve a problem.'

- What exactly was the situation?

- How did the client present the problem to you initially?

- How exactly did they say that?

- How did you respond?

- Then what happened?
- What was it about the situation that made it so frustrating for you?
- What happened in the end?

  'I am sure there are times when you have to deal with an irate customer or end-user. Can you think of a time when you really felt good about how you handled an awkward situation?'

- What exactly was the problem?
- How was it brought to your attention?
- How did they say that? Was it said in an angry voice?
- Putting yourself in their shoes, do you think their anger was justified?
- How did you approach things from that point on?
- Exactly how did you say that?
- Strategically, do you feel now that that was the right way to handle it?
- How was the situation resolved?

We're looking for the ability to put oneself in the shoes of the other person and to see things through their eyes. We're also looking for strategic insight and sensitivity in terms of how the candidate then dealt with the problem at hand.

  'I know it's sometimes difficult to get a complex idea – something technical – across to a client who lacks technical knowledge. Can you tell me about a time when you felt you did that sort of thing quite successfully?'

- What exactly was the situation?
- What was the concept that you were trying to get across?
- How exactly did you do it? Act it out a bit – pretend I'm the client . . .
- What did the client say?

- How did you know you had gotten the point across successfully?

Note the use of a mini-roleplay here. There's no better way to let the candidate know that you quite literally want to re-create past performance.

PROJECT MANAGEMENT

Suppose we're interviewing for a systems analyst. It's a busy front-line job with the very practical objective of keeping the computers up and running, developing special software applications, keeping the company abreast of new technology, and doing a lot of general-purpose trouble-shooting.

One of the things that's going to be absolutely critical to successful performance in the job is the ability to manage a heavy workload.

Multi-faceted role

It's going to be a multi-faceted workload with lots of different priorities – multiple demands on one's time, lots of different people to keep happy.

The person is going to have to maintain a difficult balance between important long-term projects and immediate and un-anticipated crises that require instant attention.

The candidate's ability to pull off this sort of juggling act is one of those things that we have to assess. We have to generate hypotheses and look for evidence to translate those hypotheses into solid predictions.

It's early in the interview. We've used a broad-brush question to get the candidate talking about the work they've been doing during the past several years. To this point, though, they haven't talked specifically about how they organise projects or deal with multiple demands on their time – which is the area we want to delve into. So we use a follow-up.

'I'd like to talk a bit now about how you organise and manage your projects. Could you tell me a little bit about how you do it?'

That's about as specific as we should be. If we ask what approach they take to keeping six or seven different projects up in the air at one time – we'll end up telegraphing what we're after.

So we keep the follow-up fairly general.

When the candidate winds down their discussion, there may be some key points that they have not properly covered. We can see that they have good planning and organising skills but can they operate effectively in a fast-moving environment where urgent demands are being thrown from all sides? To find out we use a follow-up to the follow-up. A bit narrower in scope this time. A bit more explicit.

> 'I know in my job I have a lot of different clients that I have to keep happy – and everyone seems to want their project done "yesterday". Can you think back to a time when you had a lot of programmes that had to be written and very little time to do them?'

We're asking the candidate to think back to one specific time when they had lots to do and not much time to do it.

Then come the probes, our powerful tool for fleshing out the behavioural specifics:

- When did this take place?

- How did you go about allocating your time across the different projects that had to be completed?

- Did you have to put in any overtime to get everything done?

- Were you eventually able to get all the programmes written? How did you manage it?

- How often does this sort of log-jam occur, over an average six-month period, let's say?

'When did this take place?' is a useful question to ask. Asking the candidate to pin it down underscores the fact that we are probing for specifics.

Follow-up . . . and then probe probe probe. That's the technique.

ATTENTION TO DETAIL

There are many roles in which careful attention to detail is critical to successful performance. So it's something we put on the agenda:

> 'I know that catching errors is an important part of your job. Can you think back to the error you caught during the past year that saved your company the most money?'

That's the general follow-up question that we use to direct the candidate into this area. Then come the probes:

- When did that happen?

- What exactly was the mistake or error?

- Who made it?

- Was it just a case of carelessness, do you think, or was it something else?

- How did you catch it?

- What did you do then?

- Did you take any steps to discourage that type of error in the future?

Notice that we asked the candidate to think a bit about what caused the error they were able to catch. What a person thinks, either now or at the time when the incident happened, is every bit as behavioural as what they did. So when you're probing for specifics, don't overlook *cognitive* specifics:

- What went through your mind when you saw that?

- Do you think he really meant it?

- How did you interpret that?

- Why do you think she decided not to go along with the idea?

Here's another follow-up, designed to tell us what happens when an error or mistake, despite the candidate's best efforts, does get through:

'I guess no matter how hard we try, there are always going to be a few errors that slip by unnoticed . . . What's the worst one you can think of – during the past year, let's say?'

- What exactly was the mistake or error that you let slip by?
- How often would that sort of mistake normally occur, would you think?
- How did it finally come to your attention?
- What did you say?
- Have you taken any steps to guard against that sort of thing happening again?

This last probe is important. What specific steps have they taken to prevent a repeat of the situation being described?

Next, we have a two-part question. A general, conversational lead-in followed by the much more structured request that we look in detail at one specific example.

'I know when I'm in a hurry I sometimes rush things a bit and don't give them as much care or attention as I'd like. As a result, I end up having to do the whole job over again. Does that sort of thing ever happen to you? Can you think of a specific example from the past month or so? I'd like to know how you handled it.'

- What exactly was the job or the task?
- Were you under special time pressures?
- In what way did you "rush it through" or not take enough care?
- Did you actually have to do the whole job over again?
- Has the same sort of situation presented itself again?

CUSTOMER RELATIONSHIPS

'I suppose an important part of your job, Heather, involves dealing with the public. What would you say your strengths are when it comes to dealing with people?'

That's the lead-in. Using a relatively unstructured question, we ask Heather to talk about one specific aspect of her work – her strengths in the area of dealing with the public.

A bit later, we narrow the focus down with a much more structured question and some digging. Here's both the question and the subsequent probes:

'Can you think back to the last time when you really went out of your way to do something extra for a customer?'

- What exactly was the situation?
- What did you do or say to help the person?
- How did the person respond?
- How often does this type of thing happen in, let's say, a six-month period?
- Can you think of another example?

Having asked the candidate about a positive example of dealing with the public, we can now look at the other side of things:

'I'm sure there are times when having to deal with a customer can be a real chore. Tell me about a time that was especially frustrating or difficult for you.'

- When exactly did this happen?
- What was it about the situation that made it so frustrating?
- How did you react?
- How did the customer respond to that?
- Then what happened?
- How was the situation resolved?
- Has it coloured the relationship you have today with the customer?

- How often would you say that this sort of thing happens?

Here's another combination of a structured question and probes:

> 'I'm sure there are times when you've had to say "no" to a customer . . . when they wanted something they couldn't have, or wanted you to do something you couldn't do. Can you think back to a specific example?'

- When did this happen?

- What was it, exactly, that the customer was after?

- Why couldn't you go along with that?

- How did you explain?

- What did the customer say?

- Then what did you say?

- How was it left?

MANAGEMENT STYLE

> 'Tell me a little bit about your management style, Heather.'

People usually know what 'management style' refers to, so this brief follow-up is really all that's needed to get the candidate talking.

> 'When you say "supportive", Heather, what exactly do you mean by that? "Supportive" in what sense?'

When people use terms such as supportive or hands-off, or when they talk about such things as giving people lots of autonomy, it's best to check exactly what interpretation they are applying to these commonly-used labels. Start by asking for a simple elaboration then press for some specifics:

> 'Can you give me an example of your managing someone in a "firm but fair" manner? A specific incident?'

- What exactly was the situation?

- When did it happen?
- How did you say that to them?
- How did they respond?
- What happened after that?

'Can you think of a specific situation where your management style "backfired" or wasn't quite what was needed to get the results you were after?'

- What exactly was happening in the situation?
- When was this?
- What was your initial approach to handling it?
- What response did you get?
- What happened then?
- How would you handle that same situation if it happened today?

'Are there situations in which your management style has had to be adjusted? I'm thinking of such things as month-end, when everything has to be done in a hurry, or crisis situations, or particular types of problems?'

We're still on the subject of management style but now we're narrowing it down a bit further to the issue of adjusting one's management style to suit the situation at hand. Let the candidate give you a general answer. Then narrow it down again and press for a specific example:

'Can you think back to a specific example of that happening?'

- What exactly was the situation?
- When was this?
- In what way did your normal style of managing have to be adjusted?
- What was there about the situation that you felt called for that approach?

- What eventually happened?

We're looking here for signs of intelligent flexibility. There are times when even a supportive manager has to bark out orders or take charge of things.

'When you moved into the Controller's position did your management style change in any specific ways?'

- When you say more "hands-off", what exactly do you mean by that?

- Can you give me a specific example?

- Was it a conscious change? Something you sat down and thought about?

PEOPLE DEVELOPMENT

This is an important area to delve into when we're interviewing candidates for a managerial position. How much time does the candidate spend on the development of subordinates? What approach is taken? How much emphasis is there on working with people on a day-to-day basis as opposed to relying exclusively on the year-end appraisal?

'Let's talk for a while about the role you have played in developing the people under you. I think you mentioned in your covering letter that you viewed yourself as a good developer of people . . . '

This is our general lead-in question. A bit later, we can probe for specifics.

'During the past year-and-a-half is there one subordinate in particular that you really feel was able to blossom as a result of the efforts you made as manager?'

Again, we zero in on one specific person and we start with a 'success story'. Here are some of the probes that might come in handy:

- Who exactly was this person?

- What was their job?

- What were the areas in which you felt they needed development?

- How did you work on that area? Why? What was your strategy?

- Tell me in more detail just how you discussed that with them.

Probe for specifics. If they say they had a long discussion with the subordinate, find out what they talked about. What exactly did you say? How did the subordinate respond to that? What did you say then?

'Can you think back to a time when you really put a lot of time into working with one of your people – and the person just didn't seem to respond?'

- Who exactly was the person?

- What was it, specifically, that you were trying to work on?

- What approach did you take?

- How did the person respond?

- Would you handle it differently if you could go back and do it over again?

Now – a general question. You've talked about the development of people. Now ask the candidate to summarise what they feel are the real keys to successful people development:

'In your experience, Heather, what's the real key to developing people? What is it that really makes the difference?'

And now, if you want, you can follow-up with yet another round of 'digging':

'Can you think of a specific example of where you put those principles into action?'

- Who was the person you were trying to work with?

- What were the areas that you felt that they had to work on?
- What approach did you take?
- How did he (she) respond?

12

Spotting Patterns

An ordinary conversation generally proceeds on one level. Two people sit together and talk about 'things'.

An interview, on the other hand, is a conversation with the purpose of deciding whether the candidate has what it takes to do the job. With this purpose in mind, we have to conduct the selection interview on two levels.

THE FACTUAL LEVEL

The factual level is where we discuss *facts* – be they past events, experiences, decisions, thoughts, feelings, ideas, actions, or reactions.

Our main message has been that you shouldn't just be 'gathering' surface facts at this level. You should be digging for actual behaviour.

But there's more. We've already taken a major step toward more effective interviewing, but we're still a long way from the finishing line. There's a whole other level of interviewing, and it's here that the truly professional interviewer spends the bulk of his or her time.

THE INFERENTIAL LEVEL

The inferential level is where we look for the behavioural patterns which the facts contain – and use these to predict on-the-job performance. We need, in short, to translate facts into hypotheses.

The skilled interviewer is cool, detached, discerning and analytical. Referring to their notepad from time to time, and jotting down little reminders to think about later.

An effective interviewer is skilled at creating action. What they are really after are clues as to what sort of person they are dealing with. The re-created action then becomes the data that they have to work with.

LOOKING FOR THE PATTERNS

We use the word 'personality' to refer to the patterns that show up in a person's behaviour across time and from one situation to another. Once we've re-created the person's past performance, our next task is to see if we can discover some basic patterns running through it.

These basic patterns represent the individual's 'personality' at work, and they are the key to predicting what sort of performance can be expected in the future.

FINDING WORDS TO DESCRIBE THEM

Finding words to describe these common threads is a crucial task. The challenge here is to move from observing that the candidate did such-and-such a thing to saying that they are such-and-such a type of person.

Thus, for example, we might end up saying that someone is a 'hard-driving manager' who is a 'stickler for detail' and 'doesn't suffer fools gladly'. It is not necessary that we get into such fancy descriptions as 'ego strength' and 'need for autonomy'. What counts is that we understand how the person operates.

FACTS AND HYPOTHESES

There's probably one single error that inexperienced interviewers make more than any other, and that's to gather up a lot of 'facts' about the candidate's past and yet come away from the interviewer with little or no idea of what sort of *person* they've been talking to.

We can correct that situation by looking for patterns in the candidate's past behaviour or performance, and then translating what we find into personality-type terms of the sort alluded to above.

Here are some guidelines that might prove helpful:

1. Keeping your eyes open for them

Don't let yourself get too involved in the conversation. Keep part of your mind free to spot the patterns that are there in the candidate's description of what happened. Even while you're talking with the candidate your mind should be actively searching for patterns and common threads in everything they say.

It's like being a detective. If you walk into a room, and you're looking for clues, then you'll find them. If you're not looking for clues, then you're quite likely to walk into that very same room and not see a thing.

Too many interviewers get carried away with the 'interviewing' portion of their job, almost as if they were hosting a talk show or digging up material for a newspaper article. They forget that they're supposed to be detectives as well.

2. Keeping track of your hypotheses
And that's what they'll be at this stage in the game. Hypotheses.

- Stamina?
- Long-term goals uncertain.
- Hands-off manager.
- Too aggressive?

Jot these things down on the paper you're using to take notes. If need be, divide the notepad in half and use the lefthand side to record the 'facts' of the candidate's background and the righthand side to record your hypotheses as they come to you.

Think you see a pattern there? Find a brief word or two to describe it, and then jot it down.

3. Looking for confirming evidence
When you spot a pattern in the candidate's past behaviour or performance, treat it as a 'hypothesis' until you see the pattern showing through again in some other context then go back to your original note and put a checkmark beside it.

You'll probably spot at least two or three major patterns in each candidate's behaviour, and you'll know they're the major ones because they'll all end up with three or four checkmarks beside them.

Do you see consistent signs that the person takes people at face value – and sometimes gets burned in the process? Or tackles problems very methodically and cautiously, even in situations where quick and expedient action is what's called for? Or works best in companies that are small and relatively free of red tape?

These are the sorts of patterns you're looking for. They're the very stuff of what we mean when we talk about 'personality'.

4. Building a catalogue of models

If you're hoping to spot patterns in a person's behaviour, it helps to know in advance what sorts of patterns to look for.

You should be striving to build up a catalogue of commonly found patterns that you can store away and draw upon as you're talking with a particular candidate. Start with one or two dimensions that you've come across before, or read about somewhere. Practice applying them to people until they've become second nature to you. Then add another one. And another one after that.

THE EVALUATION QUESTION

This involves asking the candidate to come up with hypotheses about their own behaviour.

For example:

You're interviewing a young graduate who has informed you that they had been elected head prefect during their final year at school. A good evaluation question might be:

'What qualities do you think your classmates recognised in you that caused them to elect you head prefect?'

Or, suppose the candidate has built up an excellent track record in a number of previous selling jobs. A good evaluation question might be:

'What is there about your approach to selling, do you think, that would account for the success that you appear to have had so far in your selling career?'

Finally, imagine talking to a candidate who has changed jobs often enough during the past several years that you think it might mean something. You might ask:

'Let's see, you've had three, four, five jobs in the past ten years . . . do you think there's any reason why you've moved around so much?'

Asked in a genuinely open-minded way, and used with a fair degree of selectivity, the evaluation question invites the applicant to go beyond the reported facts and look at the underlying factors at work.

By doing so, it presents a number of advantages to you, the interviewer.

1. It helps you formulate hypotheses

We talked earlier about the need to develop hypotheses about the candidate's skills and attributes as they are talking. The need is to relate the 'facts' of the candidate's background to the core dimensions which we are trying to evaluate. The evaluation question gives us the candidate's view of what the facts mean – of what skills and attributes underlie the specific experience and events in their background.

2. It prevents jumping to conclusions

Asking the evaluation question is a good way of making sure that we know how and why the candidate did what they had done.

It is all too easy to assume, for example, that graduating near the top of one's class means that the candidate is very intelligent. In actual fact, the posing of an evaluation question might reveal that the candidate did so well simply because they worked harder – or because the class as a whole was a mediocre one.

3. It stimulates genuine introspection

Most applicants have been interviewed before, and many have become quite good at it. It is fairly easy for the 'experienced' interviewee to run through their background in a very articulate and impressive fashion without once stopping to really think.

The evaluation question forces the candidate to stop and reflect. By doing so, it reduces the likelihood of your being unduly impressed by sheer talk alone.

BEING PREPARED TO PROBE

When you ask people to tell you about their strengths and weaknesses the answer you get is very likely to be broad and generalised to the point of being meaningless.

You can usually tell by the way these statements roll off the person's tongue that they have been well rehearsed. They're 'stock answers'.

But don't hold that against the candidate. It is preferable to have someone who's taken the trouble to prepare them than to listen to someone ramble on incoherently.

The real trouble is that these answers are so full of clichés that it's hard to put much stock in their content.

There are a couple of reasons why this happens:

- A lot of people simply aren't very good at analysing themselves crisply and incisively. They think in broad generalities, and don't spend a lot of time on introspection in the first place.

- Because they're on guard. There's an important job at stake and the way to get it is to make a 'good' impression.

- Either way, you have to be careful when you ask people for their broad evaluations of themselves. Always dig a little bit with some good follow-up probes.

  'Aggressive is a pretty broad word, what do you mean when you say you're aggressive? How might it show up, for example, in the way you manage people, or the way you handle staff meetings?'

What you're trying to do is break beyond the semantics barrier that is always there when you're talking about people's 'personalities' – and bring things down to a behavioural level where you can get the data and decide for yourself whether the person is 'aggressive' or not.

Positive or negative evaluation questions?

It's not often that you hear the candidate say anything negative about themselves when you ask a direct question:

- How did you get along with your last boss?

- How is it that you've changed jobs four times in the last seven years?

When the candidate hears this type of question, they are quick to realise that it's an important one, and that the answer is going to be looked at very carefully.

Negative characteristics are more apt to be mentioned during a discussion when the candidate feels confident than when they feel threatened.

Most of your evaluation questions, therefore, should be of the positive variety--especially during the initial stages of the interview.

> 'You were able to turn around the division a lot more quickly than anyone had anticipated . . . What do you think accounted for that?'

> 'So, at the tender age of 32, you were given responsibility for the total engineering department. What is it about you, or your performance, do you think, that led to your being selected for the role?'

Once you've asked a few of these positive evaluation questions, you're in a position to begin probing for shortcomings. Even here, though, try to do it in a fundamentally positive and accepting manner.

THE SHARED HYPOTHESIS

There's no better way of taking a tentative hypothesis and checking it out by putting it out on the table and seeing what the candidate's reaction is.

> 'You know, when I hear you talking about the way you handled yourself in that meeting, and the way you manage your own work group, it seems to me that you're not quite as aggressive as the job you're doing seems to call for.'

Or:

> 'I'll tell you what I'm concerned about at this stage. I see a lot of good traits in you, and I can see why you've made the progress that you've made over the past few years. But I have a hunch that you're a bit too much the "entrepreneur" to really be happy in this job.'

The sharing of hypotheses is an advanced technique, both in terms of how much skill is involved and when it enters into the interviewing process.

You're not accusing the candidate of anything. You're simply asking for their help in deciding whether a conclusion that's starting to emerge is one that holds water.

It's a very potent technique, especially when it's combined with follow-up probes, as we see in this example:

'As you've been talking, I've been thinking to myself – Boy, you're really an aggressive sort of individual . . . when you want something, you sure don't beat around the bush; you just put your head down and go for it. That's true, isn't it?'

And the candidate, at that point, will probably think about that for a minute and then come back with something like:

'Yes, I think that's very true of me. I don't think it's a question of being aggressive so much as it is a matter of knowing what I want. Once I know what I'm after, I get impatient with people or with things that get in my way.'

And that gives you a perfect opportunity to carry things a little further and say:

'Doesn't that get you into trouble at times? I mean, I know people who know what they're after – and they usually end up getting it – but they don't go around knocking people over or barrelling through them. They're *tactful*. And patient.'

And the candidate will then probably keep the ball rolling, and come right back with something like:

'Yes, I know what you mean. I guess I'm just not built that way. I don't believe in pussyfooting around or trying to be diplomatic just because other people are too scared or too bloody lazy to get off their rear ends and *do* something.'

Ah ha! I think we know now what sort of person we're dealing with. Let's try this on for size:

'Well, okay. But what would you do if, let's say, you were pushing for something in a staff meeting and the Chairman says "Okay, I think we've talked this one through pretty well and we're still at loggerheads . . . let's shelve it for now and put it back on the agenda for next week". How would you handle that sort of situation?'

You can see where the conversation is leading. You're getting a handle on one particular aspect of the candidate's personality, checking it out with him, and then seeing how it might show up in the new job.

This underscores the importance of generating hypotheses during the interview. Even if we don't share our hypotheses openly with the candidate, we can still validate them in the interview by searching for behavioural examples.

TAKING NOTES

Once the interview has been concluded it is essential that you have some record of what was discussed and decided.

A good interviewer does not rely on memory alone as a means of recording and storing the data. They take notes – both while the interview is in progress and immediately after its conclusion.

There are two objections to note-taking which are commonly voiced. One is that note-taking during the interview tends to create tension and caution in the person being interviewed. The other is that it is difficult for the interviewer to really concentrate on what is being said. Let's examine both of these arguments.

It generates tension and caution

This depends on how the notes are taken. If the candidate can easily see what is being written down, or if the notes are taken only when they say something negative – then anxiety and wariness are almost inevitable.

The best way to take notes is to do so evenly and unobtrusively. Keep the pad on your lap rather than on the desk, and take notes consistently but not constantly throughout the course of the interview.

It prevents genuine concentration
An experienced interviewer learns to take notes naturally and automatically, without removing their attention from the candidate and without failing to hear the real meaning of what is being said.

This comes with practice. The best approach is to develop a form of shorthand which you can easily decipher – and record only those things which are important.

Drawing up hypotheses
One approach is to take a blank pad of lined paper and draw two columns: one on the left for **facts** and one on the right for **hypotheses**.

There should be relatively little written on the facts side of the form. There is no reason to record things which are available on the application form or CV, for example.

Concentrate on writing those things which the candidate has done or said which you feel are significant. Look for specific events, actions, decisions, or experiences which you feel have a lot to say about the candidate's skills and attributes.

Most of your notetaking should take place on the hypotheses side of the form. One source of hypotheses will be your actual observations during the interview:

- Communicates clearly.
- Relates easily to strangers.
- Gets lost in detail.
- Slow to grasp things.

Another main source will, of course, be your own interpretations of the 'facts' being presented. We also have the candidate's own self-evaluations as a third fruitful source of hypotheses.

The experienced interviewer does a lot more than simply gather 'facts'. They are weighing those facts, listening for their true meaning, spitting and translating the patterns behind them into predictions about on-the-job behaviour. They are developing hypotheses. And it is these hypotheses – not the facts on which they are based – that hold the real secret to effective hiring.

13

Using an Interview Checklist

The interview with Heather is over. You have three other people to see or there's a meeting you should have been in five minutes ago.

There's a rule we should establish right here and now. *At the end of every interview, allow five minutes for note-taking.* Follow this rule religiously. Don't deviate from it.

Our purpose in this chapter is to take a closer look at the interview checklist--something you will be using to record your thoughts about the candidate.

A checklist forces us to attend to certain things. If *took the initiative in steering the discussion into specific areas* is one of the items on our checklist, then we have to look, during the interview, for this specific sort of behaviour. If we didn't have the checklist, or if we had one but this item wasn't on it, then we might not notice this specific sort of behaviour.

THINKING LIKE A CUSTOMER

As we go through the checklist, we are going to pay particular attention to how we use Heather's behaviour as an important source of data. You may recall what we said about thinking like a customer. We have to assume that how she behaves in the interview is representative of how she would behave when face-to-face with a colleague or customer. So we size up in the exact same way that a colleague or customer would do it. We pay attention to what we see and what we hear.

1. Goal orientation
She has developed the habit of setting specific and
meaningful goals for herself. ☐

She pins her goals down in clear, precise terms. She knows
exactly what she is after. ☐

She sets goals which are realistically attainable – but which involve a definite 'stretch'. ☐

She develops a specific action plan that tells her how each goal will be achieved. ☐

She attaches a specific target date to each of her goals whenever possible and appropriate. ☐

She keeps her plans out in the open. They serve as a guide to day-to-day decision-making. ☐

Winners are decisive, disciplined goal-setters. They make clear decisions about what they want and then go after it in a disciplined and well-orchestrated fashion.

It's not enough to know that a candidate is ambitious. The more important question is whether the candidate really works at it. And working at it begins with the setting of clear, specific goals. Successful people set a clear, specific goal for themselves. They attach a target date to it and know precisely what they want to accomplish.

Moreover, it becomes clear that goal-setting is a general habit that applies as much to their personal lives as to their business lives.

Give extra marks to the person who writes goals down. Experience shows that ideas floating around in one's head seldom amount to much more than daydreams, while things that are written down on paper are acted upon and get done.

2. Organisation

She plans her day systematically. She knows what has to be done and in what order. ☐

She writes down what specific goals have to be accomplished during the day. ☐

She talks in an organised way. She makes a point logically and systematically. ☐

She goes into meetings and presentations well-prepared and with a clear plan in mind. ☐

She came into this interview well-prepared. She had taken time to do her homework. ☐

She has demonstrated the ability to plan, organise, and
execute a major project.   ☐

We need to know that Heather is an organised person who gets
things done – and pursues her goals – in a systematic, intelligent,
and effective manner.
  We'll look at two things:

• how she has organised things in the past, both on the job and off

• how she has gone about organising herself for this interview.

3. Initiative

She has a strong sense of urgency – keenly aware of the
need to move quickly on things.   ☐

She seems to move into action promptly and decisively
when a problem arises.   ☐

She keeps on top of things, follows through, makes sure
that things get done.   ☐

She has shown a willingness to cut through red tape in
order to move things ahead.   ☐

She has shown initiative – taking the bull by the horns and
dealing with things.   ☐

She has shown a consistent pattern of independent
decision-making and action-taking.   ☐

Initiative is something we generally recognise when we see it. The
person does what has to be done, even if it means doing something a bit out of the ordinary.
  We look at the person's achievements – both on the job and off
– and dig for the specifics of *how* they achieved things.

4. Intelligence

Her education suggests that she is comfortably
above-average in intelligence.   ☐

She has successfully handled complex products with
complex applications.   ☐

She was thinking during the interview. She was mentally
alert, quick on the up-take. ☐

She seems quick to grasp what is being said and where the
discussion is going. ☐

She cuts quickly to the heart of a question or issue. She
sees what's crucial and what's not. ☐

She seems to have a good vocabulary. She uses words that
are not used by most people. ☐

To do an effective job a person has to have *ground-level* intelligence. A certain quickness, flexibility, and agility. The ability to think effectively on one's feet.

Does Heather grasp what you are asking – quickly, accurately, and without having it spelled out in detail? Is she alert? Does she see and respond to the gist of what you were asking even when you rambled a bit or your question turned out to be a bit clumsy?

Does she ask equally intelligent follow-up questions which show that she has actually thought about the answer you gave and is building upon it?

5. Relationship-building

I enjoyed talking with her. I can easily imagine making
friends with this person. ☐

She has a friendly manner – cheerful, outgoing, positive,
glad to see you. ☐

She seems to be socially active and to have quite a wide
circle of friends. ☐

She seems to have built good relationships with her
colleagues and/or customers. ☐

She has got to know colleagues and/or customers on
something more than just a business basis. ☐

She is easy to talk to – relaxed, able to make small talk and
keep a conversation going. ☐

We will be assessing this in our discussion of Heather's education, work history and personal life and hobbies. In many ways, however, the best evidence of a person's being able to build good relationships is the sort of impact they make on you during the interview. The candidate should be at ease, relaxed, comfortable, not self-conscious or inhibited or cautious and ill-at-ease.

If you were meeting such a person for the first time, at a party, you wouldn't have to 'make conversation' with them. It would flow naturally.

Look for signs, too, that the person exercises basic social skills – that they are a good conversationalist, good at drawing people out or using a nod of the head to express interest and encourage the other person to say more.

6. Communication skills

She communicated ideas clearly and succinctly during the interview. ☐

She stopped periodically to make sure we were on the same wavelength. ☐

She uses words effectively – using the right word or phrase in the right spot. ☐

She talks in an interesting fashion. She is an interesting person to listen to. ☐

Difficult or awkward questions were handled smoothly. She didn't get flustered. ☐

She listens well. She really pays attention and works hard to understand. ☐

What do we mean by good communication skills? Firstly, we have to look at how the person talks. Do they say things in a straightforward manner or do they over-rely on clichés and general words or phrases that don't quite fit.

Does Heather listen effectively? Do we see active, genuine listening? Does she ask us to clarify something that wasn't quite clear, and ask intelligent follow-up questions that show she has really been listening?

7. Leadership

She seemed confident and sure of herself during the interview. ☐

She stated facts and opinions in a confident and authoritative way during the interview. ☐

More than once, she took the initiative in steering the
discussion into a specific area. ☐

She gave evidence of being willing to challenge or interrupt
in an appropriate way. ☐

She took the initiative in raising the *what happens next?*
issue at the end of the interview. ☐

At various points in her life, she has been selected by her
peers for a leadership role. ☐

Heather was comfortable saying what was on her mind. Did she
state facts and opinions in a confident and authoritative manner
or did she seem tentative, hesitant, or even apologetic? Is she
definite in her beliefs and unambiguous in her opinions, or is she
vague and wishy-washy?

An assertive person, someone with leadership ability, will
gently interrupt you during the interview in order to make a point.
It will be done gracefully and perhaps with a bit of humour . . . but
it will be done.

And that same person will resist being interrupted or side-
tracked. If you interrupt they will be gracious about it. They won't
just keep talking but, when you've made your point they'll go
back to where they were before the interruption.

8. Enthusiasm

There is a 'sparkle' to her eyes when she talks. There is
enthusiasm showing through. ☐

You can tell from her voice that she is enthusiastic. It
shows in how she talks. ☐

She expressed enthusiasm about the job – and about this
company as an employer. ☐

She expressed enthusiasm about previous jobs, products, or
employers. ☐

She enjoys her work. It is clear that she really and truly
enjoys what she does. ☐

On at least one occasion, her enthusiasm was what allowed
her to achieve results. ☐

How do we know whether a person is enthusiastic? It comes from their eyes and their voice. Enthusiastic people talk in an animated manner. Their voice goes up and down to lend emphasis to what they're saying. Their eyes seem to sparkle when they talk about what they're involved in.

Still, there are times when you might want to throw in a reflective comment.

> 'I don't sense you were very enthusiastic about that particular part of your job, Heather . . .'

If she says she wasn't and then explains why, or protests and says she was enthusiastic then you've learned that either she doesn't display her enthusiasm or else what she calls enthusiasm is more of an intellectual quality than an emotional one.

Treat them as cause for concern and probe for the same sort of thing later in the interview. The sort of enthusiasm that we find in successful people is very much an *emotional* quality, not an intellectual one, and it is very much displayed in their manner.

9. Drive

She sets her sights high, not settling for 'average' or 'satisfactory' results. ☐

There is evidence that she has displayed tenacity in the pursuit of her goals. ☐

In at least one situation, she stuck with something when most people would have given up. ☐

She enjoys competitive sports, and she enjoys them because they are competitive. ☐

There is an intensity about this person. You sense it when you talk to her. ☐

She has excelled. She has succeeded in being the very best in what she does. ☐

People with 'drive' stick with a goal until it has been achieved. They are *focused*.

We can see signs of that tenacity in their educational background, or it might be a goal that they were pursuing at work.

Whether the goal was actually achieved or not is not the crucial thing; it's what went into it.

10. Resilience

She has shown evidence of being able to rebound following an important setback. ☐

She has experienced adversity. She has not had a life where everything has come easily. ☐

On at least one occasion, she has shown herself able to take criticism and learn from it. ☐

She is able to leave problems behind at the end of the day. She doesn't dwell on things. ☐

She doesn't get discouraged or dispirited when results are slow in coming. ☐

Self-confidence is one of the specific strengths she mentioned when asked. ☐

Is Heather the kind of person who has learned to deal maturely with problems, obstacles and frustrations?

Top performers are people who have aimed high and they will have had their share of setbacks and failures.

Try to talk in some detail about something Heather has attempted and failed, or a very trying experience such as the loss of a loved one or the loss of a job.

Ask what she did following the event. Did she rebound quickly, and get on with things? Did she *learn* from the experience?

11. Self-development

She has demonstrated the ability to analyse her own mistakes and learn from them. ☐

She has demonstrated the habit of analysing every sales call and learning from it. ☐

She has, and can articulate, specific self-development goals toward which she is working. ☐

She can identify in what specific ways she has improved during the past twelve months. ☐

She welcomes feedback on her own performance and takes
active steps to solicit it. ☐

She keeps abreast of industry developments, new products,
what the competition is doing. ☐

Winners are always looking for an extra edge. They see themselves as tools for the accomplishment of results. They are always
thinking about their own effectiveness, turning to self-help books,
analysing and improving their performance, trying to anticipate
what new knowledge and skills will be needed to maintain a
competitive edge in tomorrow's selling environment.

It goes beyond just taking courses. The key thing is why the
courses were selected. The best courses are those which Heather
selected herself because they were needed to enhance her effectiveness. If she had to pay for the course out of her own pocket, so
much the better.

12. Stayability

We have discussed my concerns about hiring good people
and then having them leave. ☐

She has addressed those concerns, and I feel comfortable
with how she has done that. ☐

She has a realistic view of the job – what's involved, what it
will be like. ☐

She has a realistic view of the company and what it will be
like to work here. ☐

Her long-term career aspirations can be realistically
satisfied within this company. ☐

She has demonstrated a reluctance to 'hop' from one job to
another without good reason. ☐

Will Heather stay with the company long enough to re-pay the
considerable investment of time and money we will make in her?

The question *What?* is an important one. What are Heather's
career goals? What is their perception of the job for which they
are a candidate? What is their view of your company or organisation as a place to work?

Once you have an answer to this question you can see
how closely the answer matches reality. Are Heather's career

aspirations in line with the opportunities the job contains? Is her perception of the job realistic?

Be totally candid.

> 'Heather, there's no question in my mind but that you could come in here and be a super performer. What I'm *concerned* about is whether or not we could hold on to you long enough to make it worthwhile.'

Be up-front about it. Put it out as a problem that the two of you have to find an answer for.

14

Making the Decision

To the novice interviewer, this final step in the interviewing process always appears to be the most complex and mysterious. Oddly enough, though, it's actually the easiest step of all.

It involves **visualising** how Heather will perform. Close your eyes and imagine the candidate handling the Tuesday marketing meeting, or giving a presentation to the purchasing people, or handling the telephone call that Frank had to deal with last Tuesday.

VISUALISING FUTURE PERFORMANCE

How can we conjure up a life-like image of something that doesn't yet exist?

We can because we now know Heather in the sense of having watched her perform in the past. We've heard the voice, noticed the mannerisms, seen the reaction to this or that event, observed the way in which he or she handles different situations or deals with various types of people.

Our interviewing should have allowed us to reconstruct Heather's past performance almost as vividly as if we had been there.

MAKING THE DECISION

Having projected Heather into the new job we're now in a position to ask ourselves whether we like what we see.

When we ask this question we're moving toward making a decision about the candidate. A decision to hire, to reject, to put on hold, or to ask her to come in again for another interview.

Deciding what we want to do now should come as easily.

We're not really predicting anything, as most people assume. We're simply reacting to something we've seen.

In many ways it's a decision that almost makes itself. Our task is simply to let it emerge, acknowledge it, sign the bottom line, and put it into action.

IS IT REALLY THAT SIMPLE?

Why shouldn't a hiring decision be easy? Think back to when we laid out our behavioural strategy for the interview. Imagine yourself being able to watch candidates actually perform their current jobs for one whole day.

Watch how they plan their day. Watch how they organise their time and decide what to do. Watch them as they call on people, or talk to people on the telephone, or interact with their colleagues, or talk and relate to their managers.

If you could do all this, knowing who to hire would be very easy and very straightforward. You probably wouldn't even have to think about it. The choice would be obvious.

RELYING ON 'GUT FEEL'

'Gut feel' is something that the really good interviewers and decision-makers rely a lot on yet few people are able to explain what that it is. Or how it works. Or how to go about acquiring it.

It is assumed that it can't be taught or learned or packaged for public consumption. It's something you either have or don't have.

However, we feel comfortable arguing that you can learn 'gut feel' because it is nothing more than a definable interviewing strategy and a teachable set of interviewing techniques. The same strategy and techniques, in fact, that we have been describing in this book.

The effective interviewer has the ability to go beyond the simple 'facts' of a person's background and gain insight into – or get a 'feel' for – the person themself. And then draw meaningful inferences about how well the person will perform in the job for which they are a candidate.

The really good interviewers use the process, the strategy and the techniques that we've been discussing in this book.

TRUSTING YOUR INSTINCTS

Trusting their instincts is something that all good interviewers do when the time comes to act upon what they have learned about a candidate and make a final decision.

In the interview, they probe for specific behaviour and they search for patterns in that behaviour that will tell them what sort of person they are dealing with. They then project that person into the new job and under the new set of circumstances and ask themselves how they feel about what they're watching.

So, if your instincts are telling you that Heather is the person you want to hire . . . then you should be prepared to trust those instincts and move on them.

GAUGING YOUR EXCITEMENT

You should feel excited about getting Heather on board and turning her loose. If you're not excited about it, then something's wrong. This is a big event and there's great things to come. Heather's going to be an outstanding performer, and that's going to make your customers very happy and it's going to help grow the business.

It's also going to enhance your reputation as an outstanding manager who has this wonderful knack for picking winners.

If you're feeling something other than excited and enthused, then maybe you should stop and think about it. It's a sure sign that you're not convinced that Heather is going to be an outstanding performer.

In that case you should not move ahead. Life is too short to be hiring someone about whom you are not enthused and excited.

REALISING THAT NOBODY'S PERFECT

No matter how much Heather impressed you she's not going to come in and automatically be an outstanding performer. She has to be managed.

It might be that she's not quite as aggressive as you'd like her to be in handling sales calls. She gets high marks on every other facet of the sales call, but she doesn't quite move things along as smartly as most of our top people do. It might make the

difference between her being a good performer and a top performer.

- What are you going to do about it?

- What's your plan?

- When does the plan go into action?

These are tough questions that have to be tackled as part of the
total selection process. When bringing a person on board it is
important to put together a management plan which ensures they
end up being as successful as they deserve to be.

If Heather needs to become a bit more proactive in the
sales call, you tell her that. Describe the sort of behaviour
you've seen that has led you to raise this issue and compare
that with what might produce a better result during the next sales
call.

There isn't a candidate in the world who can come in and be a
star performer without doing something a bit differently than
they've done in the past. And it won't happen unless you exercise
your managerial responsibilities. Not by signing the person up for
a training course but by talking to them. By being a coach. A
catalyst. A facilitator.

RECRUITING PROACTIVELY

One of the biggest obstacles to good hiring is the time factor. If
we're scrambling to fill a territory that's been vacant for two
months, or if we're hurrying to get someone on board in time for
the training programme then it's tough to do a really good job of
hiring.

The best way around this is by having a supply of good candidates available when we need them.

Recruiting agencies will claim it is their role to ensure that such
a supply is always available. But few of them deliver. They hound
us incessantly when we don't need someone, and then have
trouble delivering the goods when we need to get someone in a
hurry.

They don't solve the problem.

They make it worse because they lure us into forgetting that it is us – the managers – who should be operating as our own recruiting agencies.

Ferreting out the best people in the industry, getting in touch with them and keeping tabs on what they are doing and letting them know that you'd like to sit down and talk when the time is right – this has to be one of your most important priorities.

Do it . . . and you will get results.

Index